THE DOMESTIC PRESIDENCY

Policy Making in the White House

SHIRLEY ANNE WARSHAW
Gettysburg College

ALLYN AND BACON
Boston • London • Toronto • Sydney • Tokyo • Singapore

Vice President and Editor-in-Chief, Social Sciences: Sean W. Wakely
Senior Editor: Joseph Terry
Editorial Assistant: Susan Hutchinson
Marketing Manager: Quinn Perkson
Editorial Production Service: Chestnut Hill Enterprises, Inc.
Manufacturing Buyer: Suzanne Lareau
Cover Administrator: Suzanne Harbison

Library of Congress Cataloging-in-Publication Data

Warshaw, Shirley Anne.
   The domestic presidency : policy making in the White House / by
Shirley Anne Warshaw.
      p.   cm.
   Includes bibliographical references and index.
   ISBN 0-205-17538-4 (paper)
      1. United States—Politics and government—1945–1989.   2. United
States—Politics and government—1989–   3. Presidents—United
States—Staff—History—20th century—Case studies.   I. Title.
E839.5.W35   1997
320.973—dc20   96-30124
                                                                          CIP

Printed in the United States of America
10 9 8 7 6 5 4 3 2 1   01 00 99 98 97 96

For Allen,
Chris, Andy, and Bobby

CONTENTS

Preface   xi

CHAPTER 1

The Institutionalization of White House Control
of Domestic Policy   1

Overview: Nixon to Clinton   2
Institutionalization of the Domestic Policy Process   4
Emergence of an Institutional Process for Domestic Policy   5
Domestic Policy: An Institutional Part of the Presidency   11
Conclusion   13

CHAPTER 2

The Nixon Presidency: Charting a New Course   15

The 1968 Election   15
Victory: Nixon's the One   17
The Transition: A Four-Pronged Process   18
Structuring Domestic Policy in the White House   26
Reorganization: A New Domestic Advisory Structure Emerges   34
The Domestic Council Emerges   38
Policy Making in the Domestic Council   46
The Second Term   51
The Legacy in Domestic Affairs   54

CHAPTER 3

The Ford Presidency: Managing Brushfires   56

Nixon's Resignation Imminent   56
Nixon Resigns: The Transition Begins   57

The Rumsfeld White House   61
Rockefeller and the Domestic Council   66
Overhauling the Domestic Council   69
The Domestic Council without Rockefeller   75
Focusing on Brushfires   77

CHAPTER 4

The Carter Presidency: Focus on Government Efficiency   79

Campaign 1976: Setting the Domestic Agenda   81
Addressing Limited Domestic Issues   82
The Transition   83
Reorganization Examined   85
Cabinet Government   87
The Domestic Council Reviewed   87
Restructuring the Domestic Council   88
The Domestic Policy Office   90
The Triumvirate: Reviewing Reorganization   93
Carter as Public Administrator   97
Watson's Control of Policy Development   99
The Free for All: Departmental Independence in Policy Making   102
A New Approach to Policy Making   105
Conclusion   110

CHAPTER 5

The Reagan Revolution: The Conservative Agenda   111

A Foray into National Politics   112
Campaign 1980: The Revolution   114
The Transition   117
Designing the Domestic Agenda: The First Four Years   122
Cabinet Councils   125
The Legislative Strategy Group   127
Changes in the Office of Policy Development   128
Reagan's Second Term   133
Iran-*Contra* Redefines the Domestic Agenda   140
Conclusion   144

CHAPTER 6

George Bush and Company: The Caretaker Presidency 145

Campaign 1988: Set a Clear Direction 146
The Transition 150
Key Appointments: Cabinet and White House Staff 156
Creating a Domestic Policy Process 159
Marching Orders 162
Moving the Process at a Faster Clip 168
Foreign Policy Dominates the Bush Agenda 172
A Return to the Domestic Agenda 173
Baker Moves In 178

CHAPTER 7

The Clinton Presidency: The Democrats Return 179

The 1992 Election 179
The Transition 180
Setting a Domestic Agenda 187
Domestic Policy Making: Creating an Organization 193
The Domestic Agenda of 1993 197
Bringing Order from Chaos 203
Institutionalization and the Clinton White House 209

CHAPTER 8

Conclusion 212

Defining the Institutional Character of Domestic Policy 212
Comparing Management Styles for Domestic Policy 213
Politicization of the Domestic Policy Staff 214
Domestic Policy within the White House Organization 216
Summary 218

Index 221

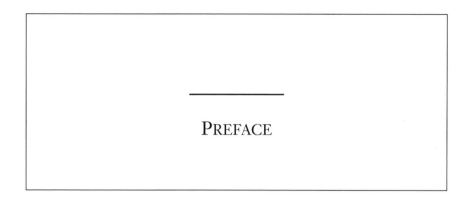

PREFACE

The study of the presidency includes a breadth of literature covering everything from campaigns and elections to presidential roles to management styles. However, the literature that focuses on organizational structures and institutional behavior within the White House is one of the weaker sections in the field of presidential studies.

This book attempts to broaden our understanding of the organizational structure and the institutional behavior of the White House staff, using the domestic policy office as a key. *The Domestic Presidency: Policy Making in the White House* examines the domestic policy office throughout six administrations, from Nixon through Clinton. The primary task of the book is to determine whether domestic policy making has become an institutionalized component of the White House staff in the modern presidency. The answer is yes. Once that question has been resolved, the study seeks to resolve how the domestic policy staff operates. Are there differences in organizational behavior from administration to administration; what is the degree of politicization of the domestic policy staffs; how is domestic policy developed; what role does the president play in shaping the domestic agenda?

I am indebted to a host of students who contributed to the research for this book. In particular Michael Strazzella, Kevin MacMillan, and Jen Cable. All three conducted interviews of White House staff members that are used in this book. Michael Strazzella interviewed staff from the Bush White House and Kevin MacMillan and Jen Cable interviewed staff from the Clinton White House. They developed the questions and conducted the interviews. Suzanne Welsh created the detailed charts throughout the book, and Matthew Diaz managed the research process as I wrote the book. I am indebted to Kim Tracey who checked all of my citations—a daunting responsibility. Finally, thanks to Eric Fritz for his assistance with the index.

At Allyn and Bacon many people contributed to the final production of this manuscript, without each of whom I could not have moved forward. Their guidance and good humor have made this a workable project. I would also like to thank the reviewers of this text, Phillip G. Henderson, Catholic University, and Raymond Tatalouich, Loyola University, Chicago.

C H A P T E R 1

THE INSTITUTIONALIZATION OF WHITE HOUSE CONTROL OF DOMESTIC POLICY

During the past fifty years, since Franklin Delano Roosevelt moved the presidency into the dominant policy role in the executive-legislative relationship, presidents have focused increased resources into managing the domestic agenda. These resources have included broadening the advisory network through task forces and commissions, augmenting departmental staff to respond to programmatic mandates, and expanding the White House staff.

This research examines one part of the president's increased role in developing and managing the domestic agenda: the White House Office of Domestic Policy, often referred to simply as the Domestic Council or Domestic Policy Council. The White House Office of Domestic Policy is responsible for establishing a domestic agenda for the administration, coordinating domestic policy throughout the administration, and prioritizing legislative initiatives. Increasingly, the White House staff has abandoned the public administration doctrine that the White House staff should be few in number, anonymous, and remain as brokers of policy rather than initiators of policy.[1] The president's domestic policy office has emerged as the core of administration domestic policy development and management and consists of a large, technically competent staff who protect the president's political and programmatic agendas.

It is the goal of this study to establish how recent presidents have used their White House staffs to frame a domestic policy, organize the often disparate parts of the administration in support of that policy, and build the coalitions of support necessary to move that policy forward. Surprisingly, each administration has chosen to organize the domestic policy unit within their White House staffs quite differently. The organizational structures vary from administration to administration as do the size of the units, the political and

[1]Richard Rose, "Organizing Issues In and Organizing Problems Out", *The Managerial Presidency*, James Pfiffner, editor (Pacific Grove, California: Brooks/Cole, 1991), p 110.

policy background of its members, and their roles in managing the general domestic policy process.

Having a structured domestic policy unit is itself a modern occurrence beginning with Richard Nixon, who was the first president to formally create a domestic policy office within the White House. Before Nixon, presidents used senior White House staff to work with the departments to guide domestic policy. Nixon, however, created an organizational unit within the White House to both develop and guide domestic policy initiatives. Every president since Nixon has followed the same path by incorporating a domestic policy unit within the White House staff. The name of the unit changes from one administration to the next, but its role remains essentially the same.

Research for this book is based on interviews with White House staff, departmental and cabinet personnel, journalists who cover the White House, reviews of archival material from presidential libraries, and a broad range of published material. All of the research covers the six administrations from Nixon to Clinton.

The foundation for this study is derived from the strong body of literature on presidential decision making and presidential management style.

Overview: Nixon to Clinton

Each of the six administrations from Nixon to Clinton has taken a different approach to developing and managing domestic policy within the White House, contributing to an ever-changing domestic policy process. The Nixon administration built a large White House staff, responsible for establishing the domestic agenda and ensuring departmental cooperation to bring that agenda to fruition. In contrast, the Ford administration shied away from a strong White House staff because of the Watergate scandal and used its domestic policy office primarily for "firefighting" and crisis management, such as the Nixon pardon. A separate economic policy unit was created to focus on rising inflation and unemployment and to deflect public attention from Nixon's Domestic Council, whose staff had been involved in the Watergate cover-up. Watergate dampened public approval for a strong White House staff and refocused public support for more departmental involvement in policy making.

President Jimmy Carter took the middle ground between the Nixon and Ford approaches to managing domestic policy. Carter created a small White House staff office that created broad goals for the administration and used ad hoc cabinet groups, known as *cabinet clusters*, to define objectives. Ronald Reagan, who had captured the presidency from Jimmy Carter by a significant majority, scrapped most of the Ford and Carter structures and returned to the Nixon structure of a large, policy-oriented White House domestic office that established general objectives for the administration. He expanded the Nixon structure by reducing the role of the departments in both defining and refining policy and, instead, used the departments as "bully pulpits" for White House strategies.

Eight years later, the Bush administration again reframed the domestic policy process. The deep-rooted enmity between the Bush and Reagan supporters led to a complete overhaul of the domestic policy office when George Bush took the reins of government. Bush, who sought to capture public support for his presidency through foreign affairs, reduced the domestic policy office to "firefighting" status and legislative liaison work. Agenda-setting, policy management and departmental coordination were not key parts of the Bush domestic policy operation. The director of the domestic policy office rarely saw the president and eventually had two levels of staff above him.

After George Bush lost his reelection bid to Bill Clinton, Clinton again restructured the White House domestic policy office. The role of domestic policy management was split into two units, one for domestic policy and one for economic policy—a dual approach reminiscent of the Ford years. The return of the White House to Democratic hands after twelve straight years of Republican control led to another overhaul of the domestic policy process. Not only did the Clinton Democrats want to purge the personnel, but they also wanted to create a structure that encouraged a team approach to policy development. Building on the cabinet cluster idea of the Carter administration, the Clinton staff devised a domestic policy structure that relied on White House–departmental teams for policy initiation and management.

This ever-changing role of the domestic council has contributed not only to a lack of continuity in domestic policy but often a certain chaos in the domestic policy office as well. Events such as Watergate, personality clashes such as between Reagan and Bush, and political conflict such as between Bush and Clinton have contributed to the failure to bring consistency to the domestic policy process. The absence of either a continuing structure or continuing staff in the management of domestic policy has been reflected in severe problems that each administration has faced in framing a domestic agenda and building both legislative and public support for that agenda. Three administrations (Ford, Carter, and Bush) failed to secure a second term, one (Clinton) is uncertain about securing a second term, and one (Nixon) was forced from office. Only one (Reagan) of the six administrations survived two full terms. Not surprisingly, only the Reagan administration built a strong domestic policy office, studied the lessons of past administrations, and wove strong alliances with the departments.

Although the problems that the domestic policy office had in each administration may be only one factor in the failure to gain public support in their re-election bids, it remains a significant factor. Failure to gain control over the White House domestic policy structure is a failure to gain control over the domestic policy process.

Institutionalization of the Domestic Policy Process

The absence of continuity in either the domestic policy office or in the formulation of domestic policy is part of the discussion on the institutionalization of the domestic policy process. Do we acknowledge that because every president since Nixon has established a domestic policy unit within the White House that we now have an institutional process for policy development? That leads to the broader question of what we mean by the term *institutionalize.* Have we institutionalized a presidential press secretary or a congressional liaison or national security advisor because every modern president has had one?

Erwin Hargrove sought to answer these questions over two decades ago as he grappled with the definition of the institutional presidency. For Hargrove, "the presidency has thus become an institution with enduring characteristics that continue across time despite changes in the person of the president."[2] Those characteristics included the functional compartmentalization of expert staffs, such as the legislative liaison, national security staff, and domestic policy staff.

The discussion on the institutional parts of the institution of the presidency was similarly tackled by Richard Neustadt, who defined institutionalization as whether an organization or procedural innovation survives a change of administration from one party to another.[3] Phillip Henderson refined Neustadt's definition to distinguish a change from party to party to a change in administration. According to Henderson, "As organizations and procedures designed to assist the President are emulated by successive administrations, a process of institutionalization unfolds."[4]

The test established by Hargrove, Neustadt, and Henderson refers to any organizational unit within the White House that is consistently reconstituted by succeeding administrations. Harvey Mansfield provides greater depth to the definition by requiring "the emergence of a patterned response" to the issues at hand.[5] For Mansfield, the test of an institutionalized process

[2]Erwin C. Hargrove, *The Power of the Modern Presidency* (New York: Alfred A. Knopf, Inc., 1974), p 81.

[3]Richard Neustadt, "Staffing the Presidency: Premature Notes on the New Administration," *Political Science Quarterly*, vol. 93, Spring 1978, p 2.

[4]Phillip Henderson, *Managing the Presidency: The Eisenhower Legacy from Kennedy to Reagan* (Boulder, Colorado: Westview, 1988) p 14.

[5]Harvey C. Mansfield, "Reorganizing the Federal Executive Branch: The Limits of Institutionalization," *The Institutionalized Presidency*, Norman C. Thomas and Hans W. Baad, editors (Dobbs Ferry, New York: Oceana Publications, Inc., 1972).

would involve a domestic policy office that provides a routinized process for dealing with domestic issues. One would speculate that such routinization for Mansfield would include the routinization of White House–departmental processes and the routinization of internal White House processes.

Perhaps the most detailed analysis of the issue of institutionalization of White House policy units emerged in John P. Burke's *The Institutional Presidency*. Burke establishes three criteria for institutionalization:

1. First, an institution is organizationally complex both in terms of what it does (its functions) and how it operates (its structure).
2. Second, an institution is generally universalistic and routine in its decision making and operating procedures.
3. Finally, an institution is well bounded and differentiated from the larger environment in which it is situated.[6]

Burke further notes that for a White House unit to be institutionalized it should have centralization of control over the policy-making process, centralization of power within the staff in one or two key aides, and routines that are typical of bureaucratic organizations.[7] To a large extent, Burke has built on Hargrove's thesis of institutionalization that similarly provides for expertise within the staffing unit, hierarchical decision making within the unit, stratification of rank within bureaucratic structures, and continual rivalry between functional units for presidential attention.[8]

Therefore, the essence of an institutional unit for domestic policy would be one that recurred from administration to administration, had a continual presence within White House decision making, involved a staff with certain hierarchical qualities and bureaucratic functions, and whose primary responsibility was consistently focused on domestic policy. The test for institutionalization of domestic policy within the White House focuses on the recurring role of a policy unit within the White House to manage, to a greater or lesser degree, the president's involvement in the administration's domestic agenda.

Emergence of an Institutional Process for Domestic Policy

The existence of an institutional process for domestic policy is one that has been evolving for over seventy years, even before Franklin Delano Roosevelt aggressively sought to control the national agenda through the creation of

---

[6]John P. Burke, *The Institutional Presidency* (Baltimore, Maryland: Johns Hopkins University Press, 1992), p 27.
[7]Ibid., p 35.
[8]Erwin C. Hargrove, *The Power of the Modern Presidency*, p 81.

the Executive Office of the President. Although presidents throughout the eighteenth and nineteenth centuries had worked with their department heads in devising a policy agenda, presidents had little control over departmental initiatives. Whether departments remained in line with presidential goals often depended on the personal relationship of the president to the department, a relationship frequently strained by cabinet appointments made in haste or through political necessity.

The evolution of presidential involvement in the formulation of domestic policy has involved four distinct phases: the earliest phase that focused on presidential rather than departmental management of federal expenditures; the second phase that involved presidential review of departmental policy initiatives; the third phase that sought to frame domestic policy using a network of outside task forces; and finally the emergence of a White House structure for management of the administration's domestic policy agenda.

Phase One: Central Legislative Clearance

As the twentieth century moved into full gear, the federal government began an era of unprecedented deficit spending. After twenty-eight years of budget surpluses, the nation exploded with six straight years, from 1904–1910, of budget deficits.[9] Deficit spending forced a reappraisal of the process used for creating and managing the national budget. Throughout the nation's history, the Treasury Department had been responsible for transmitting the federal budget to Congress by assembling departmental budget requests into a Book of Estimates. Neither the Treasury Department nor the president had authority to ensure a balanced budget or to provide a coordinated agenda.

This process changed in 1921 in response to the 1912 Taft Commission on Economy and Efficiency that recommended that the president prepare and coordinate a comprehensive program for the budget. Hampered by the crisis that emerged in the European theater and the explosion of a world war, the legislation did not move through Congress for another nine years. In 1921 Congress reexamined the Taft Commission report and passed the Budget and Accounting Act of 1921, providing for the establishment of a Bureau of the Budget (BOB) within the Treasury Department, headed by a director appointed by the president.

The Budget and Accounting Act of 1921 provided the president the institutional mechanism for reviewing departmental budgets and ensuring that each budget met presidential objectives. Those budgets not in line with

[9]See Larry Berman, *The Office of Management and Budget and the Presidency, 1921–1979* (Princeton, New Jersey: Princeton University Press, 1979) for an excellent study of the Bureau of the Budget and its successor, the Office of Management and Budget.

presidential objectives were deleted or revised. The concept of presidential management of the domestic agenda through budgetary means was expanded in the Roosevelt era. To ensure complete programmatic consistency within the federal budget, Roosevelt appointed former federal judge Samuel Rosenmann to develop a broad administration strategy for domestic affairs. His role included working with the departments in a manner similar to those roles played by White House staffers Harry Hopkins, who worked with the State Department in diplomatic affairs, and Admiral William Leahy, who worked with the military agencies. Similarly, Truman appointed Clark Clifford as special counsel, responsible for broad domestic policy formulation and John Steelman as assistant to the president, responsible primarily for labor/management issues.[10]

Thus, by the Eisenhower administration, a formal process for presidential clearance of departmental legislative submissions had become systematized through the Bureau of the Budget, and a White House staff had emerged to develop broad guidelines for domestic policy. The institutionalization of the domestic policy process within the White House was well underway in the 1950s.

The emergence of a structured process for presidential control over departmental budget submissions to Congress focused the need for broader presidential control over the policy process itself. Without a coordinated plan for managing the domestic agenda, the tools for budgetary control were only minimally useful. Eisenhower's small White House staff was ill equipped for the task. As Larry Berman noted, "the President or his closest aides had to personally integrate and coordinate the program recommendations with budgetary policy."[11] To address this problem and recommend solutions, Eisenhower created the President's Advisory Committee on Government Organization (PACGO), chaired by Nelson Rockefeller. PACGO was charged with exploring new ways for the Executive Office of the President to manage both budget and policy coordination.

PACGO recommended improving the president's in-house advisory structure for integrating administration policy goals with the budgetary process through the addition of a Director of Administration on the White House staff. Budget Director Percival Brundage saw the move as a threat to BOB's authority and actively opposed the new position. For Brundage, creation of such a White House position would threaten the ability of the BOB to work directly with the president. Eventually Brundage succeeded in fending off any reorganization of the Bureau of the Budget's authority into the White House.

---

[10]See Stephen Hess, *Organizing the Presidency* (Washington, D.C.: Brookings Institution, 1988) for a detailed study of White House staff from Roosevelt to Reagan.

[11]Larry Berman, *The Office of Management and Budget and the Presidency, 1921–1979*, p 59.

Phase Two: Task Forces and Commissions

The seed that PACGO had planted for increased White House involvement in managing and coordinating the policy and budgetary process continued to grow in the Kennedy and Johnson years. Kennedy, as Lester Salaman notes, saw the presidency "as exceptionally well equipped to reject or modify departmental initiatives, but not to seize the policy initiative on its own where agency timidity or the need for a multi departmental approach was necessary."[12] Rather than fight another battle with the Bureau of the Budget over creation of a White House policy unit, Kennedy and Johnson pursued an ad hoc policy advisory system using networks of outside advisors, task forces, and commissions. Task forces were the primary advisory structure, however, since the nature of commissions required a public report.[13] A public report negated some value of the advisory process, since it allowed the report to be subjected to interest group, departmental, and congressional scrutiny before the White House had marshalled its own political networks. Task forces, whose reports remained within the confines of the White House, became the more preferable advisory structure.

The use of task forces and commissions to provide policy advice was still considered to be ineffective, resulting, in 1966, in the creation of the President's Task Force on Government Organization, headed by Ben W. Heineman, president of the Northwestern Railway. Heineman's seven-member team recommended a greater presence for the White House in developing broad policy objectives. Its recommendations were never implemented because of Johnson's decision not to seek reelection in 1968.

Phase Three: Assistant to the President for Domestic Policy

Similarly concerned with the absence of a structured in-house process for managing the expanding responsibilities of the federal government, Richard Nixon appointed the five-member Advisory Council on Executive Organization, under the direction of Litton Industry President Roy L. Ash. As had the Heineman Commission, the Ash Council was charged with devising organizational structures within the Executive Office of the President for overseeing the expanding federal bureaucracy.

The council was given a budget of $930,000 and was directed to complete its work by the end of the year. As directed, the Ash Council swiftly completed its work. Within twelve months, the Ash Council had completed Reorganization Plan 2 of 1970. Sent to Congress by Nixon on March 2, the

[12]Lester Salaman, "The President and Policy Making", *Analyzing the Presidency*, Robert E. DiClerico, editor (Guilford, Connecticut: Dushkin Group, 1985), p 213.
[13]See Thomas R. Wolanin, *Presidential Advisory Commissions: Truman to Nixon* (Madison, Wisconsin: University of Wisconsin Press), 1975.

plan gained bipartisan support and quickly passed into law. Reorganization Plan 2 provided for the first formal structure within the White House for managing the domestic policy process.

The cabinet-level Domestic Council was established by the Reorganization Plan to ensure coordination of domestic programs and to reduce duplication of programmatic efforts. The Domestic Council was viewed by the Ash Council as a group that would collectively discuss with and propose domestic policies to the president. In a sense, this recommendation used the task force approach of the 1960s but minimized the inherent problems that task forces faced. Because task forces were composed of outsiders, their recommendations often lacked an institutional memory or an understanding of implementation constraints and political inconsistencies. The Domestic Council offered the benefits of a task force but without the limitations.

Although the Domestic Council provided broader policy input to the president than either the Bureau of the Budget or the task forces provided, management of the domestic policy process remained outside the White House. As the first formal step toward moving management into the White House, Nixon built on PACGO's recommendations from a decade earlier for an Assistant to the President for Administration and created the Assistant to the President for Domestic Policy. John Ehrlichman, a senior member of Nixon's staff, was named to the position and given responsibility for coordinating the Domestic Council's activities.

Creation of a White House position to oversee domestic policy was the first major step toward institutionalization of a White House process for domestic policy management and control. To deflect criticism that one office would manage the entire range of domestic policy, Nixon created a series of White House offices including drug abuse prevention, consumer affairs, energy, and the aged.

The movement toward a centralized domestic policy process in 1970 began the process of institutionalizing management of domestic policy within the White House. Each successive administration continued to have a senior staff member with the title Assistant to the President for Domestic Policy, who in turn had a sizable staff to manage departmental activities and to develop new initiatives. The Bureau of the Budget, that had been renamed the Office of Management and Budget as part of the 1970 Ash Council recommendations, remained the primary source of fiscal management and, to a greater or lesser degree, worked with the White House domestic policy staff to ensure that new initiatives met budgetary considerations.

Phase Four: Restraining White House Control

White House control of domestic policy grew yearly under John Erhlichman's control of the domestic agenda. Ehrlichman established a process for reviewing departmental programs for consistency with the broader administration domestic agenda and worked in concert with departmental staff to develop new initiatives. Departments cleared every major activity with the White House, including speeches on domestic programs.

By the end of his term, Nixon had centralized the domestic policy process and established the White House as the focal point for coordination and initiation of the domestic agenda. However, the powerful White House staff that managed domestic policy was also involved in the massive cover-up of the Watergate break-in of the Democratic National Committee. The Watergate affair not only brought down the president, but brought down the White House staff as well. Gerald Ford sought a major restructuring of his relationship to the departments by restoring policy independence to the departments and reducing White House control of policy development. The Ford model was one of broad White House guidance without control. At his first cabinet meeting, only hours after Nixon's resignation, Ford directed his cabinet not to work through the Domestic Council or White House staff, but to work directly with him.[14] According to Ford, "A Watergate was made possible by a strong chief of staff and ambitious White House aides who were more powerful than members of the Cabinet but who had little or no practical or political experience or judgment. I wanted to reverse the trend and restore authority to my Cabinet...I decided to give my Cabinet members a lot more control."[15]

The restructuring of control over domestic policy development did not diminish the institutional role for the White House staff in domestic affairs. Ford continued to have a senior staff member to oversee, although to a lesser degree than had Nixon, domestic policy, and he continued a formal White House-cabinet relationship through the Domestic Council. The institutionalization of White House management of domestic policy was continuing.

The Carter years became another marker for the institutionalization process, for Carter also continued to have a senior staff member oversee domestic policy and to have a formal White House-cabinet relationship. Rather than using the Republican-created Domestic Council, however, the Carter staff utilized a series of ad hoc cabinet groups, known as cabinet clusters, to work with White House staff in the formulation of domestic polices. The White House continued to forge the total agenda within which departmental initiatives evolved.

Although the Carter staff operated in the middle ground between the Nixon and Ford White House staffs, by the end of the Carter administration the departments themselves were seeking greater White House involvement

[14]Memorandum for the President, transition team, August 10, 1974, Box 62, Philip Buchen Files, Gerald R. Ford Library, Ann Arbor, Michigan.
[15]Gerald R. Ford, *A Time to Heal* (New York: Harper & Row, 1979), pp 131–132.

in the domestic process. Two departmental assistant secretaries, Ben Heineman, Jr. and Curtis Hessler, wrote that there should be "larger, more institutional staffs" in the White House to "guide the development and implementation of presidential-level issues."[16] The pressure of a burgeoning federal government and the necessity of substantive policy guidance to that government was forcing creation of administrative structures within the Executive Office of the President. The institutionalization of a domestic policy process was essential for an activist and strategic presidency.

Phase Four: Re-establishing White House Control

The Reagan years marked a return to a strong White House presence in domestic policy, with the creation of the cabinet council structure. As Heineman and Hessler had suggested, stronger administrative procedures needed to be established for domestic policy management. During the Reagan administration, those procedures involved a White House domestic policy staff that not only forged the broad agenda but ensured that departmental initiatives met certain criteria established by the White House using the cabinet councils. Through the Office of Policy Development, the Reagan White House guided the cabinet councils toward policies that satisfied the general political and programmatic goals of the administration.

The abbreviated Bush presidency continued the Reagan structure, although the departments were allowed greater latitude in policy management than they had been under the Reagan White House. Under Bush, the White House often abdicated policy control to the Office of Management and Budget, who sought to cut domestic programs almost across the board.

The process of institutionalizing domestic policy management within the White House continued in the Clinton administration. The White House again created a domestic policy office with senior staff to forge a policy agenda and to ensure departmental consistency with that agenda. Under Clinton, the domestic policy advisor reports directly to the president, has a large, technically competent staff, and is responsible for working with the departments to create specific policies that meet the broad policy agenda.

Domestic Policy: An Institutional Part of the Presidency

The previous discussion has focused on the development of a consistent process throughout the past fifty years for White House management of domestic policy. The theme throughout this discussion has focused on the evolving

---

[16]Ben W. Heineman, Jr. and Curtis A. Hessler, *Memorandum for the President: A Strategic Approach to Domestic Affairs in the 1980's* (New York: Random House, 1980), p 11.

White House process and eventual institutionalization of domestic policy management as a role within the White House staff.

The definition of institutionalization focuses on a process whose characteristics endure from administration to administration. The primary characteristics of the institutionalized domestic policy staff can be identified as a formal White House staff unit, with a bureaucratic organizational structure, and a routinized process for interacting with the departments. Every White House, from Nixon through Clinton, has maintained a formal White House staff unit for managing domestic policy. Each of those units has also maintained a large staff within the White House, with clear lines of hierarchical authority within the unit. Each domestic policy office has had a director, associate director[s], and various subunits with staff.

While the title of the unit has changed in most administrations, its function has remained the same. The role of each domestic policy office has been to forge a broad domestic policy agenda and to ensure that the departments are cognizant of that agenda in their policy proposals. The degree to which the domestic policy office interacts with the departments and the process used for that interaction is the least institutionalized part of the domestic policy process.

This lack of institutionalization in the domestic policy process is not likely to improve, because it touches the heart of the question of political power and legitimate authority. For the White House to manage the domestic policy agenda and ensure departmental consistency with that agenda, department heads must support the White House staff and have confidence in its ability to handle the job. Department heads must approve of the legitimate authority of the White House staff to move the president's agenda forward.[17] Such authority is premised on department heads' accepting clearly defined presidential goals and objectives and moving toward their implementation. This acceptance of White House staff authority is premised on a shared sense of commitment to presidential objectives, a commitment based on personal loyalty, political ideology, or a combination of both.

Cabinet acceptance of the legitimate authority of the White House staff therefore depends on a White House staff with clearly formed, well-articulated goals and objectives as established by the president, and similarly depends upon a cabinet committed to those goals and objectives.

Two different problems mitigate the likelihood of the institutionalization of a process for White House-departmental interaction. First, in order to gain broad-based public support in their election, Presidents rarely develop well-defined policy agendas. The less well-defined a policy proposal is during

---

[17]See D. H. Wrong, *Power* (New York: Harper, 1979) for a detailed discussion of legitimate power and legitimate authority.

an election, the more support it will garner. As a result, the test for institutionalization established by Hargrove perhaps best defines the domestic policy unit. As defined by Hargrove, the very compartmentalization of policy responsibilities is a test of institutionalization. Burke's refinement of this definition would suggest that the White House has institutionalized domestic policy if the domestic policy unit involves the centralization of power for policy development, has a hierarchical and bureaucratic structure, and involves a continuing relationship between the departments and the White House for policy development. The only characterization of an institutionalized process that the domestic policy office does not meet is that identified by Mansfield, that calls for a patterned response to the issues. Although routinized mechanisms for dealing with domestic policy issues have not been established as Mansfield calls for, the domestic policy office responds to issues as mandated by the sources of power inherent in the governing process. The degree to which the White House exercises legitimate authority will control the consistency of patterned responses to the issues. Since the exercise of legitimate authority is an inconsistent process, the ability to establish patterned responses will be similarly inconsistent. The absence of a routinized structure for policy management, however, does not negate the institutional quality of the domestic policy office.

Conclusion

The White House office of domestic policy, a unit that has continuing responsibility for managing the president's domestic policy agenda, has emerged as an institutional part of the president's advisory and management structure. Its evolution has spanned seventy years, beginning with the Bureau of the Budget's transformation in 1921 to a central clearinghouse for departmental budget submissions to Congress and including a continuing effort by presidents to create an in-house advisory structure for domestic policy.

The emergence of a formal White House unit during the Nixon administration culminated the movement toward a formal domestic policy structure and resulted in the institutionalization of domestic policy making. The existence of a domestic policy office in every administration since Nixon meets the definition of institutionalization as a process that continues from administration to administration, whatever party, and includes the existence of a formal unit with bureaucratic structures and procedures. The absence of continuing methods for White House-departmental interaction or for internal discussion of policy does not impede the nature of the institutionalization of the domestic policy process.

In essence, the domestic policy office has been institutionalized within the White House. Its name will vary, its relationship to the departments will vary, its internal structures will vary, but its function as the primary determinant of the administration's domestic agenda and the primary coordinator of domestic policy within the administration will remain constant. The test of institutionalization is a test of functional and organizational consistency, both of which are met by the domestic policy office. As Richard Neustadt noted, a simpler test of institutionalization is the recurrence of "separate telephone numbers, letterheads, histories and futures" within the White House.[18] The White House staff has become a series of separate, and generally institutionalized, units with different responsibilities, different constituencies, and different operating behavior. The domestic policy unit joins a wide range of White House staffing units as an institutionalized component of the White House and, to larger degree, the managerial presidency.

---

[18]Richard Neustadt, *Presidential Power* (New York: The Free Press, 1990), p 219.

CHAPTER 2

THE NIXON PRESIDENCY:
CHARTING A NEW COURSE

After twenty-two years in politics, including two runs for the presidency, Richard Milhous Nixon finally captured the White House in 1968.[1] His 1960 loss to John F. Kennedy triggered an eight-year odyssey to regain the White House and to return policy making to Republican control.

Nixon's drive for the presidency in 1968 focused primarily on ending the war in Vietnam, a war that had bitterly divided the nation and brought down Lyndon Johnson's administration. Domestic issues were secondary to the 1968 campaign strategy as the war dominated the campaign rhetoric. When domestic issues were of necessity addressed, Nixon attacked the Johnson administration's problems with crime and portrayed a nation beset with a breakdown in law and order. Nixon was able to frame the campaign around the issues of his choice.

Hubert Humphrey, Johnson's vice president and the Democratic standard bearer, was not only hampered by his reluctance to attack the policies of Lyndon Johnson, but by a party deeply divided during the Democratic primaries. The Democratic Party had been torn by challenges from Eugene McCarthy and Robert F. Kennedy, both of whom opposed Johnson's Vietnam policies. The internal strife within the Democratic Party had drastically diminished the party's ability to rebuke the Republican challenge.

The 1968 Election

Humphrey's chances of winning the 1968 election were further complicated by the third party challenge of Alabama Governor George Wallace. Wallace

---

[1]Nixon began his political career by defeating incumbent Democrat Jerry Voorhis for California's twelfth House district in 1946. He then won the 1950 election against Helen Gahagan Douglas, for the newly vacated seat of Sheridan Downey, to become California's junior senator. In 1952, Nixon was selected by Dwight David Eisenhower to be his vice presidential running mate.

campaigned solely on domestic issues, addressing, primarily, civil rights issues and the national government's movement to desegregate southern schools. Wallace had gained broad support in the deep south and was making major inroads into the traditional blue-collar Democratic vote in the industrialized northeast. Humphrey was forced to respond, allowing Nixon to continue his attacks on the administration's foreign policy.

Wallace and his American Independent Party became a serious contender for the nomination and tried to force both Nixon and Humphrey to deal with the volatile issues surrounding civil rights. Nixon's strategy was to avoid civil rights and the Wallace candidacy as much as possible and to narrow the debate to Johnson's policies on crime and the war in Vietnam. Crime, a nondivisive issue that generated broad-based support, became the primary focus of Nixon's domestic policy speeches. As often as possible, Nixon prefaced his speeches with "Humphrey, a do-nothing candidate on law and order" as he sought to focus the election on the narrow, domestic debate on crime. A typical campaign speech would include such general statistics as "There has been one murder, two rapes, forty-five major crimes of violence, countless robberies and auto thefts..." Although the statistics were essentially accurate, Nixon was playing on the nation's growing concern over crime that stemmed from the riots and looting that erupted after the 1968 Democratic convention and the urban unrest in the aftermath of Martin Luther King's slaying.

Nixon's Foreign Policy Focus

Although Nixon focused on crime as the core of his domestic agenda, foreign policy and particularly the war in Vietnam remained the overall theme of the 1968 campaign. As he noted in his acceptance speech at the Republican convention in Miami Beach, "I pledge to you tonight that the first priority foreign policy objective of our next Administration will be to bring an honorable end to the war in Vietnam." He jabbed Humphrey with constant references to the Johnson administration's failure to end the war and denounced the Democratic ticket as being too closely aligned with the Johnson policies to change the course of the war.

Nixon's focus on foreign policy involved not only the war in Vietnam, but issues of conventional and nuclear weaponry, the Middle East, and detente with the Soviet Union. To a significant extent he was successful in narrowing the agenda to foreign policy, but occasionally his facts failed the test of accuracy. In an October 24, 1968, radio address, Nixon charged that the Kennedy and Johnson administrations had allowed the Soviet Union to gain the advantage in strategic weapons. Nixon attacked Humphrey for contributing to "a gravely serious security gap." But Humphrey turned the tide on Nixon, noting that "we have three times as many strategic nuclear weapons in our strategic alert forces as we had at the end of the [Eisenhower] administration, including a fifteen-hundred percent increase in the number of ballistic missiles."[2]

The "security gap" lapse did not seriously damage Nixon's campaign, and he continued to focus the debate on foreign policy rather than domestic policy. There was, as Stephen Ambrose noted of the Nixon campaign, a "relative indifference to domestic affairs."[3] Humphrey found himself on the defensive on Vietnam and the escalation of the Cold War, and he allowed Nixon, for all intents and purposes, to ignore the domestic agenda. Nixon's failure to concentrate on domestic issues was rationalized during the campaign by the statement that "domestic problems... will be easier to solve with the war over."[4] In reality, however, it was Nixon's total lack of interest in domestic affairs that kept the campaign in the arena of international affairs and national defense. As Nixon loyalist Leonard Garment noted, "The basic Nixon need was to keep the home front tranquil while large foreign policy strategies" were pursued.[5]

Victory: Nixon's the One

Nixon's running mate, former Maryland governor Spiro Agnew, played an almost nonexistent role in the 1968 campaign.[6] The campaign rarely referred to the "Nixon/Agnew" ticket, referring instead to the "Nixon" ticket. Most campaign literature had only a large picture of Nixon with the words "Nixon's the One" prominently displayed across the bottom. Agnew rarely gave major speeches or made campaign appearances, and he was generally relegated to speaking in the border states where he had a moderate following. He was charged with ensuring that Maryland and Tennessee were firmly in the Nixon camp on election night.

Humphrey was eager to capitalize on Agnew's lack of participation in the campaign and, not surprisingly, frequently included his running mate, Senator

[2]Tom Wicker, *One of Us: Richard Nixon and the American Dream* (New York: Random House, 1991), p 367.
[3]Stephen E. Ambrose, *Nixon: The Triumph of a Politician 1962–1972* (New York: Simon and Schuster, 1989), p 171.
[4]"Nixon Administration Takes Shape: The Course Charted," *U.S. News and World Report*, December 23, 1968, p 19.
[5]Interview with Leonard Garment in *The Nixon Presidency: Twenty-Two Intimate Perspectives of Richard Nixon*, p 104.
[6]One explanation for Nixon's choice of Spiro Agnew, a relative unknown in national Republican circles, was that he did not want to be overshadowed by his vice presidential running mate. During the 1960 election, his running mate, Henry Cabot Lodge, was referred to as more presidential than Nixon.

Edmund Muskie of Maine, in his campaign appearances. Humphrey, in almost mocking terms, compared the broad experience of Muskie in national affairs to the limited experience of Agnew. The press contributed to the mocking of Agnew by referring to Muskie as "Lincolnesque," because of his physical appearance, which was similar to that of Abraham Lincoln.

Although Humphrey had tried to stop the Nixon bandwagon, the war in Vietnam proved to be the undoing of his campaign. Neither the caustic Agnew strategy nor the Johnson/Humphrey domestic achievements could overcome the reality of a war that was costing the lives of thousands of Americans, with no end in sight. Even the administration's last-minute announcement of peace talks in Paris failed to convince the American public that peace was at hand. By election day on November 5, Nixon had successfully marshalled an electoral majority to win the presidency, capturing 301 electoral votes to Humphrey's 191 electoral votes and Wallace's 46 electoral votes. The popular vote, however, was far closer. Not until 8:30 A.M. the next morning when Illinois was finally certified in the Nixon column was Nixon declared the winner in the national news media. Nixon had edged out Humphrey with less than 1% of the vote, garnering 45.4% (31,770,237) to Humphrey's 42.7% (31,270,533) and Wallace's 13.5% (9,906,141).[7] The combined Nixon and Wallace vote, over 58% of the total vote cast, had soundly repudiated continued Democratic control of the White House. For Nixon, it was a mandate.

Nixon spent election night at New York's elegant Waldorf-Astoria, with only a few campaign staff. His wife, Pat, and their two daughters, Julie and Tricia, were given their own suite from which to follow the returns. Nixon's propensity to withdraw within a small circle of advisers, even to the exclusion of his own family, would follow him into the White House as he developed his operational structure.

The Transition: A Four-Pronged Process

With victory in hand, Nixon and a small group left the next evening for Key Biscayne, Florida, staying in a beachfront home rented from Senator George Smathers. The Key Biscayne Seven included the seven senior members of the presidential campaign: H. R. "Bob" Haldeman, John Ehrlichman, Bryce Harlow, Robert Finch, Herbert Klein, Murray Chotiner, and campaign chairman John Mitchell. These staff members were the core of Nixon's campaign, and then would emerge as the core of his presidency. Each had stood

---

[7]Wallace's announcement on October 2 of General Curtis LeMay, an advocate of the nuclear bomb, as his running mate damaged his credibility in the election. Wallace lost support after the announcement.

The decision to assign specific responsibilities to senior staff, rather than the wider-ranging responsibilities of the Kennedy and Johnson administrations, was carefully designed by Nixon. Nixon asked General Andrew Goodpaster, who had served as Eisenhower's chief of staff after the resignation of Governor Sherman Adams, for advice on structuring the White House staff. Goodpaster worked with Nixon on the White House staffing issues throughout December after the cabinet had been chosen and publicly presented. He recommended that Nixon return to the Eisenhower model of several key assistants with authority to manage specific policy areas.[24] Nixon supported that concept and later wrote that "a lean staff with a few top notch people, each of whom has an important exclusive assignment, works far better than a flabby staff where too many people have too little to do."[25]

In addition, Goodpaster recommended that Nixon return to the Eisenhower-era cabinet secretariat, which had been dormant in the Democratic administrations. Goodpaster argued that the cabinet secretary would provide the president greater oversight of departmental activities and could track presidential directives to the departments. Finally, Goodpaster encouraged Nixon to revise the decision structure to allow for multiple options to be brought to the president. Rather than a simple yes or no to White House staff or departmental recommendations, Goodpaster urged that the president be given several options to decide domestic policy from within, as presidents had been given through the National Security Council's decision structure.[26]

By the time the transition team had completed its work, the cabinet and White House staff had been selected, an organizational structure for the White House was in place, and an agenda had been broadly prepared for the new administration. The conflicts that would soon emerge within the White House centered on narrowing the domestic agenda and establishing priorities and implementation strategies. Although the task forces had provided broad goals and objectives for the administration, they had not identified those objectives that should be addressed first, nor did they identify specific means for implementing those objectives. But it should be noted here that the absence of clear priorities for the new administration was less the fault of the task forces than of the campaign itself. A survey after the election by *U.S. News and World Report* of the 1968 campaign promises listed only a "crackdown" on crime, federal revenue sharing with state government, ending the

[24]Garry Wills described the functional assignments of the Nixon staff in less cordial terms. Wills saw functional assignments as Nixon's move to filter the policy process and reduce the options that were available to him. See *Nixon Agonistes: The Crisis of the Self-Made Man* (New York: Signet Books, 1969), p 373.

[25]Richard Nixon, *In the Arena: A Memoir of Victory, Defeat and Renewal*, p 270.

[26]Interview with Andrew Goodpaster. Goodpaster was in Europe immediately after the election and did not return until early December, 1968. He met with Nixon over the course of the next six weeks at both the Pierre Hotel and at Key Biscayne, Florida.

Job Corps and encouraging private anti-poverty projects, and increased use of block grants rather than categorical grants-in-aid for local governments as domestic initiatives.[27] Nixon's 1968 campaign had deliberately focused on the war in Vietnam and the promise of peace rather than on domestic issues.

Structuring Domestic Policy in the White House

Once in office Nixon focused his administration on foreign policy, as he had repeatedly promised throughout the campaign. He was determined to end the war in Vietnam, replace confrontation with the Soviet Union with detente, halt the escalation of nuclear arms, reduce tensions in the Middle East, and forge diplomatic relations with the People's Republic of China. As Elliot Richardson, who held two cabinet posts in the Nixon administration noted, "The President's real concerns were in foreign policy and geostrategy," and he intended to focus the administration in those areas.[28]

During the transition Nixon pointedly told William Rogers, his choice for secretary of state, that he intended to manage foreign policy from the White House and to operate as his own secretary of state.[29] Rogers' role would be to carry out directives from the White House. Henry Kissinger, as national security advisor, would serve as the president's primary advisor in foreign affairs as director of a revitalized National Security Council and would act as the president's conduit to the departments of State and Defense. Nixon's determination to manage foreign policy from the White House was based both on his own preoccupation with foreign policy and, according to Kissinger, with his lack of confidence in State Department staff who "had no loyalty to him."[30] Since the majority of State Department personnel were members of the career civil service or foreign service, Nixon had few chances for replacing staff. The recourse for which he opted was to abandon the State Department's advisory structure and establish his own structure in the White House under Kissinger.

Daniel Patrick Moynihan: The Urban Affairs Council

There was, however, no obvious mechanism for managing domestic affairs within the White House. The White House did not have an institutionalized

---

[27]"What Nixon Will Do As President," *U.S. News and World Report*, November 18, 1968, p 34.

[28]Comments by Elliot Richardson in *Richard Nixon: Politician, President, Administrator*, edited by Leon Friedman and William F. Levantrosser (Westport, Connecticut: Greenwood Press, 1991), p 137.

[29]Seymour M. Hersh, *The Price of Power: Kissinger in the White House* (New York: Summit Books, 1983), p 32.

[30]Henry Kissinger, *White House Years* (Boston: Little, Brown and Company, 1979), p 11.

domestic policy structure as it had for national security policy. Domestic policy had been haphazardly managed in the White House since Franklin Roosevelt first created presidential assistants in 1939. Nixon sought to change the haphazard nature of domestic policy advising, and he established the first in-house advisory structure for domestic policy: the Council for Urban Affairs. Nixon's first official act as president was to sign the executive order on January 23, 1969, that created the Council for Urban Affairs.[31] Although limited in scope to urban issues, Nixon viewed the Urban Affairs Council (UAC) as the domestic equivalent to the National Security Council.[32]

Daniel Patrick Moynihan, an expert in urban poverty on the joint faculty of Harvard and the Massachusetts Institute of Technology, and a former assistant secretary of labor in the Kennedy administration, was brought into the White House as director of the Urban Affairs Council.[33] He was given the title Assistant to the President, on par with other senior White House staff, paid at the top level, and assured direct access to the president. Although Nixon had failed to bring a Democrat into the cabinet, he had succeeded in bringing one to the White House.

Moynihan was charged with working with the department heads, as part of Nixon's commitment to cabinet government (in domestic affairs), to develop strategies for the plight of urban America. The Urban Affairs Council would address two key campaign issues, crime and welfare, and would indirectly provide material to deal more effectively with civil rights issues. Although the war in Vietnam had moved civil rights issues out of the national spotlight, in Nixon's view they were sure to reappear. Desegregation issues in the South had already begun to surface as problem areas for the fledgling administration.

The executive order specified that the Council for Urban Affairs, as it was officially designated, would "advise and assist the President with respect to urban affairs . . . and include assisting the President in the development of a national urban policy, promoting the coordination of Federal programs in urban areas, encouraging cooperation between all levels of government, and encouraging local decisionmaking." And to ensure that the White House was prepared for urban riots and civil rights demonstrations, the executive order added in the last line that the council would "assist the President during emergency situations or under conditions threatening the maintenance of civil order or civil rights."[34]

[31]Executive Order 11452, July 23, 1969. Although the executive order designated a Council for Urban Affairs, the more frequently used term was Urban Affairs Council.

[32]Richard Nixon, *RN: The Memoirs of Richard Nixon*, p 342.

[33]Nixon asked Moynihan to join the White House staff as director of the yet-to-be created Urban Affairs Council during the transition.

[34]"Council for Urban Affairs: Statement by the President Signing Executive Order Creating the Council," January 23, 1969, Weekly Compilation of Presidential Documents.

Moynihan became the executive secretary of the council, as provided in the executive order and worked with the cabinet officers in the council to prepare a national urban policy. The executive order provided for the president to preside over meetings of the council, and the vice president to preside in the president's absence. In addition to the president and the vice president, the nine-member Urban Affairs Council included the attorney general, and the secretaries of Agriculture; Commerce; Labor; Health, Education and Welfare; Housing and Urban Development; and Transportation (Figure 2.3).

Moynihan wasted no time in making the council a working unit.[35] Immediately after the White House press briefing on January 23 on the creation of the Urban Affairs Council, Moynihan took the podium and announced the formation of nine subcommittees of the council, each of which would be chaired by a cabinet officer (Figure 2.4). Moynihan also announced a tenth

- ◆ President
- ◆ Vice President
- ◆ Attorney General
- ◆ Agriculture
- ◆ Commerce
- ◆ Labor
- ◆ Health, Education and Welfare
- ◆ Housing and Urban Development
- ◆ Transportation

Figure 2.3   The Urban Affairs Council

- ◆ The Future of the Poverty Program
- ◆ The Future of the Model Cities Program
- ◆ Minority Business Enterprise
- ◆ Welfare
- ◆ Crime
- ◆ Voluntary Action
- ◆ Internal Migration
- ◆ Surplus Food and Nutrition
- ◆ Mass Transit
- ◆ The Transition to Peacetime Economy at the End of the Vietnam War

Figure 2.4   U.A.C. Subcommittees, 1969

[35]According to John Ehrlichman, Moynihan was brought to Nixon's attention by Robert Finch, who urged that Moynihan be brought onto the White House staff to manage urban affairs. See John Ehrlichman, *Witness to Power: The Nixon Years* (New York: Simon and Schuster, 1982), p 245.

subcommittee, not directly related to the work of the other nine subcommittees, which would be supervised by budget director Robert Mayo on the transition to a peacetime economy at the end of the Vietnam war.[36]

Cabinet chairs of each of the subcommittees were expected to assign departmental staff to work on the policy issues and to prepare position statements. Moynihan assigned one member of his small staff of six to each of the subcommittees to provide a liaison to the White House. Several staff were assigned more than one subcommittee. Preparation of the final policy statement, however, often included the recommendations of task forces assembled by the subcommittee chairs. These task forces were composed of outside experts and academics, in the same vain as Arthur Burns's transition task forces had been assembled. The advice of think tanks such as the Brookings Institution was also pursued by the subcommittees and included in the recommendations.[37] Using task forces for advice was a natural outgrowth of the trend begun during the Johnson years and allowed both the agency and the Urban Affairs Council to keep their staffing requirements at a minimum.

The small Urban Affairs Council staff included senior staff member Stephen Hess and five assistants: Richard Blumenthal, Christopher DeMuth, Michael Monroe, John Price, and Leonard Zartman (Figure 2.5). Hess was

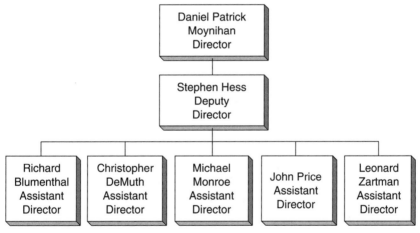

Figure 2.5   Urban Affairs Council Staff

[36]The public papers of the president list the subcommittee's title as "plans for the transition to a peacetime economy at the end of the Vietnam conflict." Moynihan lists the title as "... end of the Vietnam war." In 1969, when the subcommittees were formed, the designation of the war as a conflict or a war had not been resolved.

[37]On May 1, 1969, Nixon ordered all White House staff and cabinet not to use the Brookings Institution for policy studies due to their liberal orientation. See memorandum from Ken Cole to H. R. Haldeman in Bruce Oudes, editor, *From the President: Richard Nixon's Secret Files* (New York: Harper and Row, 1989), p 29.

given the newly created title "Deputy Assistant to the President for Urban Affairs," and each of the other five became staff assistants to the president for urban affairs. In keeping with Nixon's discussion with Goodpaster during the transition, White House staff were given job titles with specific job assignments.

While the subcommittees were poring over the policy options and preparing policy papers, Moynihan was focusing his energies on the administration's welfare reform package. Moynihan's determination to move the welfare plan forward was partly based on his own deep commitment to the program and partly on the realization that Nixon would not commit funding to many of the initiatives that the subcommittees were looking at. Welfare reform appeared to be one of the few domestic agenda items that Moynihan believed could be moved forward.[38]

The welfare package itself was divided into two parts. The first part, which the Urban Affairs Council welfare subcommittee was working on, was based on Richard Nathan's sixty-three page welfare transition task force report that recommended improving public assistance for the poor, blind, and disabled. Nathan's recommendations were based largely on a 1967 proposal by New York Governor Nelson Rockefeller, for whom Nathan had worked.[39]

The second part of the welfare reform package involved restructuring the delivery of services and cash assistance to the needy. The task force had been directed at its first meeting on December 6, 1968, not to recommend any expensive negative income tax proposals.[40] Moynihan, however, favored a guaranteed annual income—or negative income tax—and directed his attentions to preparing a proposal for minimum federal standards that Nixon would accept. By January 31, 1969, Moynihan had prepared a twelve-page memorandum to Nixon that said that "tinkering with the present welfare system is not enough. We need a complete re-appraisal and redirection of programs."[41] Moynihan urged that Nixon move forward with a guaranteed annual income. The subcommittee on welfare, chaired by Robert Finch of HEW, supported Moynihan's proposal and on February 6 moved to recommend that a "Federal floor for assistance payments" be made directly by the federal government.[42] The Moynihan-Finch proposal, however, was met by immediate opposition from Arthur Burns and his assistant, Martin Anderson.

---

[38]Haldeman notes on March 11, 1969, that "Moynihan points out that he can't have a domestic program. Not any money available." H. R. Haldeman, *The Haldeman Diaries: Inside the Nixon White House* (New York: G. P. Putnam's Sons, 1994), p 19.
[39]Joan Hoff-Wilson, "Outflanking the Liberals on Welfare," *Richard Nixon: Politician, President, Administrator*, edited by Leon Friedman and William F. Levantrosser, p 85.
[40]Op. cit.
[41]Joan Hoff-Wilson, "Outflanking the Liberals on Welfare," *Richard Nixon: Politician, President, Administrator*, edited by Leon Friedman and William F. Levantrosser, p 85.
[42]Op. cit.

Arthur Burns: Domestic Policy Advisor

While Moynihan had been given oversight for managing urban policy, Nixon had given Arthur Burns oversight for general issues of domestic and economic policy. Nixon's strategy in having two domestic advisors, Moynihan and Burns, was, as H. R. Haldeman noted, "to bring some recognition of the arguments from the other side [Democratic]...so that we would not fall into completely ingrown concepts."[43] It also allowed Nixon to have the kinds of competing policy options available to him that Andrew Goodpaster had recommended during the transition.

Burns's appointment to the White House staff was somewhat more haphazard, however, than Moynihan's had been. Although Nixon had decided during the transition to create an Urban Affairs Council and to name Moynihan to head it, he had never quite decided what role Burns would play on the White House staff. According to Burns, Nixon at one point during the transition offered him the position of chief of staff, although there is little corroborating evidence for this. It is more likely that Nixon wanted to appoint Burns to the Federal Reserve Board, but in the absence of an open position needed a holding position for Burns. When Moynihan accepted the Urban Affairs Council position, a logical spot for Burns became the White House domestic and economic advisor, in light of his tenure in the Eisenhower administration and his management of the domestic task forces. For Nixon, Burn's appointment would also provide a conservative balance to Moynihan's liberalism.[44]

Burns describes the White House job offer as occurring on January 21, 1969, when he went to the White House to discuss the transition reports in more detail.

> On January 21, when I arrived there [the White House], I still refused to take any position in the Nixon administration. I should say that we did talk about the Federal Reserve position, but at that time the position was not open. After I handed Mr. Nixon my transition report, he took me into the Cabinet room and showed me a chair. He said, "This is your Cabinet chair." It had my name on it, "Counselor to the President"...He asked me if I would come to a Cabinet meeting the next day and present my transition report to the Cabinet. I said of course I would.

Nixon's decision to move Burns into the newly created cabinet-level position of "Counsellor to the President" was also meant to signal Burns's preeminence among White House staff. The title "Counsellor" was suggested by Robert F. Ellsworth, a former congressman from Kansas and a member of Nixon's

---

[43]Interview with H. R. Haldeman in *The Nixon Presidency: Twenty-Two Intimate Perspectives of Richard Nixon*, edited by Kenneth W. Thompson, p 77.
[44]Richard Nixon, *RN: Memoirs of Richard Nixon*, p 342.

campaign staff. Ellsworth suggested to Nixon that Burns be given the rank of counsellor, a generalist who would advise Nixon on domestic and economic issues.[45] Burns' position was not only cabinet-level, as none of the others were, but was conspicuously listed first in the White House staff directory.

When Nixon announced the appointment of Arthur Burns on January 23, 1969, he stated that Burns would "head up a small group whose prime responsibility will be the coordination of the development of my domestic policies and programs."[46] The president then had two domestic policy advisors: Moynihan and Burns. Although Nixon had told Moynihan during the transition that the Urban Affairs Council would be "the domestic policy equivalent of the National Security Council in foreign affairs,"[47] there seemed some doubt after the appointment of Burns whether that would actually be the case.

Moynihan, who believed he had been given sole charge of urban affairs, pushed the departments to produce policy papers that could be merged into a national urban policy. But while Moynihan was busy with his urban strategy, Burns began pursuing the task force recommendations that he had presented to Nixon. In a series of "presidential directives" that began on January 30, Burns sent the department heads assignments to prepare policy papers on specific task force recommendations. For example, the secretary of Transportation was directed to review the supersonic transport system; the secretary of Labor was directed to recommend improvements in the unemployment compensation system; and the secretary of Health, Education and Welfare was directed to develop proposals for establishing eligibility for public assistance. Each of the directives was based on a recommendation prepared by Burns' transition task forces. Nixon had gratefully accepted the task force reports but never provided feedback to Burns. Burns took Nixon's lack of response as an approval for the recommendations and promptly began assigning cabinet officers the responsibility for pursuing the recommendations. Cabinet officers were now answering to two White House staff members for domestic policy—to Moynihan for the Urban Affairs Council subcommittees and to Burns for implementing the task force recommendations through the presidential directives.

Competing Advisory Structures

The addition of Burns to the White House staff at the last minute created two distinct and often conflicting structures for managing domestic policy.

[45]Rowland Evans, Jr. and Robert D. Novak, *Nixon in the White House: The Frustration of Power* (New York: Random House, 1971), p 18.
[46]"Statement Announcing the Appointment of Dr. Arthur F. Burns as Counsellor to the President," January 23, 1969, Public Papers of the President.
[47]Richard Nixon, *RN: Memoirs of Richard Nixon*, p 342.

Although Nixon had carefully crafted his foreign policy structure with Henry Kissinger at the helm in the White House, he had put his domestic policy structure together haphazardly. The original concept of a domestic policy operation focused on the Urban Affairs Council, which would parallel the responsibilities of the National Security Council, fell apart once Burns was added to the White House staff.

The two competing advisory structures of Moynihan and Burns were complicated by Nixon's delight at pitting the two against each other. Moynihan's liberal proposals pitted against Burns' conservative response.[48] Nixon would call Burns to the Oval Office to discuss a Moynihan proposal, which Burns would usually find fault with, and, similarly, would call Moynihan in to discuss a Burns proposal, with a similar result. The paper trail produced by Burns and Moynihan is almost comical to read.

In a memo to Nixon from Burns discussing Moynihan's suggestions for a message to Congress on urban affairs, Burns says, "I have some reservations about the message proposed by Dr. Moynihan" and proceeds to develop nine pages of urban strategies that Nixon should use.[49] In a memo to Nixon from Moynihan on the poverty program, Moynihan says, "Dr. Burns told me of your concerns on [media] coverage of the poverty program," implying that Burns had provided inaccurate information.[50] The memo expands on the successes of the poverty program and discounts Burns' information. Both Moynihan and Burns began trying to outdo each other, each trying to gain the president's confidence.

By the fall of 1969, the responsibilities of Burns and Moynihan for domestic policy had blurred. Burns became directly involved in Moynihan's Family Assistance Plan, fervently lobbying against the proposal that provided for a federally subsidized guaranteed family income. Moynihan, largely at Nixon's urging, had become involved in broader domestic programs within the departments. Moynihan's dabbling in departmental issues threatened Burns' oversight of the presidential directives that required specific agency action.

Nixon not only set up conflicting structures within his own staff, but he further diluted the ability of either Burns or Moynihan to oversee the domestic agenda by creating a series of other domestic policy units. On May 29,

---

[48]For a discussion of the Moynihan-Burns relationship see exit interview of John Whitaker, May 4, 1973, White House Central Files, p 8–9, Nixon Presidential Materials, College Park, Maryland.

[49]Memorandum for the President from Arthur Burns, "A Program for the Cities," March 17, 1969, Box 16, White House Central Files, Council on Urban Affairs Folder 1969–1970, Richard M. Nixon Presidential Materials, College Park, Maryland.

[50]Memorandum to the President from Daniel Patrick Moynihan, untitled, February 20, 1969, Box 16, White House Central Files, Urban Affairs Council Folder, Richard M. Nixon Presidential Materials, College Park, Maryland.

1969, the Cabinet Committee on the Environment was created; on November 13, 1969, the Council for Rural Affairs was created; on December 23, 1969, Martin Anderson was added to the White House staff as Special Consultant to the President for Systems Analysis, to dissect federal programs and determine their cost effectiveness; and on January 1, 1970, the Council on Environmental Quality was created. Each was responsible to the president through John Ehrlichman, who had been given oversight of domestic activities that were not directly under either Moynihan or Burns.

The blurring of line responsibilities for managing the domestic departments meant increased tension within the White House and increased competition for the president's time. By the summer of 1969, neither Burns nor Moynihan had produced a significant package of domestic initiatives. In a nationally televised speech on August 8, 1969, Nixon identified his domestic agenda, named the New Federalism, and focused on four elements: welfare reform, comprehensive job training and placement, revamping the Office of Economic Opportunity, and revenue sharing. However, little progress was made on any of the four agenda items and no consensus was reached within the White House on the keystone of the plan, welfare reform.

Reorganization: A New Domestic Advisory Structure Emerges

Burns' and Moynihan's failure to capitalize on the brief honeymoon period and their constant bickering finally convinced Nixon to restructure his domestic advisory system. In contrast to Henry Kissinger's smoothly running and well-oiled machine in national security policy, the domestic policy apparatus was in shambles. John Ehrlichman described the move away from Burns and Moynihan in a conversation that Nixon had with Roy Ash.

> Nixon asked Roy Ash, "Why do I have to put up with this on the domestic side. There's got to be a more orderly way of going about the development of domestic policy than this. Henry never bothers me like this. Henry always brings me nice, neat papers on national security problems and I can check the box. Nobody badgers me and picks on me. But these two wild men on the domestic side are beating me up all the time." So they went off and devised the Domestic Council.[51]

Nixon's decision to restructure the domestic policy apparatus in the fall of 1969 did not happen quite as suddenly as Ehrlichman suggests. Rather, the domestic policy structure evolved from a series of recommendations during the Eisenhower administration to restructure the Executive Office of the President and to create a more efficient White House staff. The concept of

[51]Interview with John Ehrlichman in *Twenty-Two Intimate Perspectives of Richard Nixon*, p 124.

restructuring the Executive Office of the President had been reviewed in the 1950s through the President's Advisory Committee on Government Organization (PACGO).[52] The focus of PACGO had been to improve the general management activities of the Executive Office, particularly those in the Bureau of the Budget.

The Office of Executive Management

By 1958, the Bureau of the Budget had countered PACGO's reviews by aggressively developing their own management recommendations. Budget Director Maurice Stans recommended to Eisenhower that an Office of Executive Management (OEM) replace the Bureau of the Budget to highlight the management functions of the Budget Bureau.[53] Although the Office of Executive Management was never implemented in the Eisenhower administration, the concept of improving the organizational structure of the Executive Office and Bureau of the Budget organization was resurrected by Nixon early in his term.

Nixon had campaigned on a pledge to streamline government. He proposed creation of a Commission on Government Reorganization in a CBS radio speech on June 27, 1968, "to set in motion a searching, fundamental reappraisal of our whole structure of government...not to dismantle government, but to modernize it."[54] The issue was a priority one for Nixon as he discussed options for structuring his administration. Even on the flight from California to New York on election day, Nixon discussed reorganization with staffers Robert Finch, John Ehrlichman, and H. R. Haldeman.[55] During the transition, Nixon began his "reappraisal of government," as he called it, by establishing a task force to study a reorganization of the executive branch chaired by Frank Lindsey (President of ITEK Corporation). Lindsey's fifteen member task force concluded that the first order of business to streamline the government at large was to streamline the Executive Office of the President and the White House staff.

The transition task force was followed after Nixon took office by the President's Advisory Council on Executive Organization (PACEO) with Roy Ash of Litton Industries as chair.[56] Ash had prepared his own 10-page transi-

[52]The President's Advisory Committee on Government Organization (PACGO) was created by executive order four days after Eisenhower's inauguration. For a detailed discussion of PACGO during the Eisenhower years, see Bradley Patterson, "White House Staff Structure", *Reexamining the Eisenhower Presidency*, edited by Shirley Anne Warshaw (Westport, Connecticut: Greenwood Press, 1993), p 38–39.

[53]Larry Berman, *The Office of Management and Budget and the Presidency, 1921–1979*, p 64.

[54]Don Oberdorfer, "Agencies' Makeup Studied," *Washington Post*, April 6, 1969, p A1.

[55]Theodore H. White, *Breach of Faith* (New York: Reader's Digest Press, 1975), p 172.

[56]The President's Advisory Council on Executive Organization was created on April 5, 1969.

tion report to the president-elect during the transition entitled "Executive Office Organization," which recommended creation of an Office of Executive Management (OEM).[57] Ash's Office of Executive Management was premised on the PACGO recommendation that an Office of Executive Management be created. According to Ash,

> What we did in the whole of our work there was not to come up with any novel ideas. There had been so many people that had plowed this ground before us...OEM went back to Eisenhower's administration if not earlier...In fact, that was the title he put on it in his administration.[58]

Ash enlarged on the PACGO recommendation by urging that the new Office of Executive Management not only encompass the duties of the Bureau of the Budget but add a Division of Evaluation, a Domestic Policy Council, and a Division of Program Coordination.

The Ash Council Recommendations

The Ash Council, as it came to be known, reviewed a number of options for reorganizing the Executive Office of the President and, on August 20, 1969—barely four months after its creation—presented a formal recommendation to Nixon. That recommendation provided for creation of the Office of Executive Management (OEM) to replace the Bureau of the Budget and for the creation of a Domestic Policy Council. Nixon approved the recommendations and, on March 12, 1970, sent Reorganization Plan No. 2 to Congress, seeking approval for a new Office of Executive Management and a Domestic Policy Council. The plan was approved by Congress with a slight change in the name from the Office of Executive Management to Office of Management and Budget.

When Nixon had reached the point of removing Burns and Moynihan, he was not totally without options. Although the Reorganization Plan did not go to Congress until March, 1970, Ash and Nixon had met throughout the spring and summer of 1969 to discuss reorganization plans. By the fall of 1969, when Nixon was ready to remove Burns and Moynihan, the concept of the Domestic Policy Council had been reviewed by Nixon and Ash and had been thoroughly discussed between Ash and John Ehrlichman. In fact, the original concept for the Urban Affairs Council had been premised on Ash's recommendations during the transition that urged Nixon to restructure the

[57]Ash's task force report concluded that the president had become a "domestic desk officer" and recommended a restructuring of policy making. See John Robert Greene, *The Limits of Power: The Nixon and Ford Administrations* (Bloomington, Indiana: University of Indiana Press, 1992), p 52.
[58]Interview with Roy Ash by John Robert Greene. Author provided with copy of interview by Dr. Greene.

White House into a policy-making rather than an operational body. According to Ash, "the White House should be spent in policy making not operational activities.... The White House should be given over to managing policy, managing and carrying out policy making."[59] The Urban Affairs Council was designed not only to create the domestic equivalent of the National Security Council, as Nixon explained in his formal statement, but also to move the White House domestic operations into a policy-making process, as Ash had recommended.

The failure of the Urban Affairs Council to generate a significant amount of policy initiatives, and the failure of Moynihan and Burns to act cooperatively, did not deter Nixon from continuing to move the White House to the center of domestic policy making for the administration. Rather than brood over the failure of the operation, Nixon went back to the plan proposed by the Ash Council in August, 1969, and created a White House policy-making unit focused on the broad spectrum of domestic affairs.

In a major restructuring of the White House staff in November, 1969, Nixon dismantled the Urban Affairs Council and transferred Moynihan to a newly created White House position of "Counsellor to the President" with unspecified advisory responsibilities.[60] Haldeman noted in his daily diaries that Nixon had "decided to make Moynihan a Counselor to P., with Cabinet rank. Really best way to position him. Gets him out of operations and into free-wheeling idea-generating, plus working as prod to all others, good use of great talent."[61] Clearly Haldeman was a Moynihan fan and perhaps contributed to Nixon's decision to continue Moynihan on the White House staff in another role.

Arthur Burns was removed from his wide-ranging domestic policy responsibilities and given similar unspecified advisory responsibilities. However, soon after the reassignment of duties, Burns left the White House. In January, 1970, Burns succeeded William McChesney Martin as chairman of the Federal Reserve Board. John Ehrlichman was moved from "Counsel to the President" to a newly created White House position of "Assistant to the President for Domestic Affairs." Both Burns' and Moynihan's staffs were assigned to Ehrlichman, who became the sole voice for domestic policy in the White House.

---

[59]Interview with Roy Ash by John Robert Greene. Author provided with copy of interview by Dr. Greene.

[60]Moynihan left the White House in 1970 to return to Harvard University. In 1973 he left Harvard to accept an appointment as ambassador to India, where he remained until May 1975, at which time President Ford appointed him chief U.S. Representative to the United Nations. Moynihan returned to Harvard in February, 1976, to maintain his tenure and in November, 1976, won a U.S. Senate seat from New York.

[61]H. R. Haldeman, *Haldeman Diaries: Inside the Nixon White House*, p 96.

Ehrlichman was the logical choice for the new domestic affairs position, for the White House liaison to the Ash Council had been Ken Cole from Ehrlichman's staff. All of the memos generated by the Ash Council to Nixon were reviewed by Ehrlichman before being passed on to Nixon.[62] Although Ehrlichman did not change any of the memos themselves, he did add his own thoughts to the Ash recommendations. Ehrlichman had strongly supported the creation of the Domestic Council and a White House domestic policy staff, although he had never suggested any role for himself.[63]

The Domestic Council Emerges

The creation of an institutional domestic policy operation began in January, 1969, with the Urban Affairs Council and took another step forward in November, 1969, with the formalization of a senior staff member with the title Assistant to the President for Domestic Affairs. In November, 1969, John Ehrlichman became Nixon's chief domestic advisor, with authority over the entire spectrum of domestic decision making.

By December, Ehrlichman had consolidated all domestic-policy activities in the White House, built a staff composed of the merged Burns and Moynihan operations, and had assigned that staff to oversee departmental policy making.[64] (Figure 2.6) As Ehrlichman was gearing up his domestic affairs operation during the late fall of 1969 and early winter of 1970, the Ash Council was putting the final touches on its report to the president. The report formally recommended a domestic policy unit in the White House and the creation of a cabinet-based Domestic Council.

By March the report was completed, and on March 12, 1970, Nixon submitted the report, Reorganization Plan No. 2, to Congress. The reorganization plan, based on the Ash Council's (PACEO) recommendations, called for the creation of a Domestic Policy Council in the White House, to parallel the National Security Council, and the establishment of an Office of Management and Budget. While the Domestic Policy Council would be a new entity, the Office of Management and Budget would replace the Bureau of the Budget and would address the concerns of the Ash Council in its recommendation for an Office of Executive Management.

---

[62]Dom Bonafede and Jonathan Cottin, "Nixon, in Reorganization Plan, Seeks Tighter Rein on Bureaucracy," *National Journal*, March 21, 1970, p 624.

[63]Interview with John Ehrlichman.

[64]In an internal White House memo, it was noted that "John Ehrlichman's operation covers the whole range of domestic affairs." Memo From Lamar Alexander to BeLieu, et al., January 22, 1970, Box 1, Domestic Council FG 6–15 Folder, Nixon Presidential Materials, College Park, Maryland.

Figure 2.6 White House, Senior Staff, 1970

However, the reorganization plan was met with immediate skepticism in the Congress, forcing the White House to clarify the specifics of each of the two new units, particularly the role of the Domestic Council. In a memo written in May, 1970, to Representative John Blatnik, chairman of the Subcommittee on Executive and Legislative Reorganization, to clarify how the Domestic Council would operate in the White House, the White House explained that the Domestic Council would bring together cabinet officers to discuss major domestic policy issues and to minimize interagency conflicts over policy initiatives. According to the White House,

> the Council is intended as a forum within which the President can more readily and systematically secure the advice of appropriate department heads on important policy issues, particularly those involving the formulation of the policies and programs of one department which have a significant impact on the closely related programs of other departments. It is a forum in which options are to be

compared and the consequences of the various options can be weighed by these department heads in the presence of the President who has the difficult task of deciding.[65]

Congress ultimately approved the reorganization plan, effective July 1, 1970, in essentially the same form that Nixon had requested.

Nixon's proposed Domestic Council involved a cabinet-level group that met regularly to ensure that domestic programs were coordinated and that addressed the administration's domestic objectives (Figure 2.7). Chaired by the president, the membership of the new Domestic Council included the vice president, the attorney general, and the secretaries of Treasury; Interior; Agriculture; Commerce; Labor; Health, Education and Welfare, Housing and Urban Development; and Transportation. In addition, the director of the Office of Economic Opportunity and the postmaster general would serve on the Domestic Council. Every member of the cabinet, except the secretaries of Defense and State, sat on the Domestic Council.[66]

The plan called for the cabinet members to divide into sub-groups to prepare a "streamlined, consolidated domestic policy" using the resources of the White House to provide a staff. According to the reorganization plan, "the Council will be supported by a staff under an Executive Director who will also be one of the President's assistants. Like the National Security Council staff, this staff will work in close coordination with the President's

- ◆ President
- ◆ Vice President
- ◆ Attorney General
- ◆ Treasury
- ◆ Interior
- ◆ Agriculture
- ◆ Commerce
- ◆ Labor
- ◆ Health, Education and Welfare
- ◆ Housing and Urban Development
- ◆ Transportation
- ◆ Office of Economic Opportunity
- ◆ Postmaster General

Figure 2.7   Domestic Council,
March 12, 1970

[65]Letter from Dwight Ink to John Blatnik, May 4, 1970, Box 1, Domestic Council FG 6–15 Folder, Nixon Presidential Materials, College Park, Maryland.
[66]The President's Message to the Congress Transmitting Reorganization Plan No. 2 of 1970, Implementing Recommendations of the President's Advisory Council on Executive Organization, March 12, 1970.

personal staff but will have its own institutional identity."[67] The plan also called for the Domestic Council to take over the responsibilities of the Urban Affairs Council and the Rural Affairs Council.[68]

The Urban Affairs Council (UAC) had been the blueprint for the Domestic Council, for the UAC had been built around the concept of small groups of cabinet officers, working in subcommittees, analyzing policy proposals and coordinating departmental activities. Roy Ash's suggestion to Nixon during the transition that the Urban Affairs Council could serve to coordinate urban policy resulted in the first formal White House domestic policy unit. The lessons learned during the brief lifetime of the Urban Affairs Council provided the foundation for the larger Domestic Council and for the White House operation that supported it.

John Ehrlichman's domestic affairs office was assigned by Nixon to serve as the staff for the Domestic Council. Ehrlichman immediately moved to restructure the relationship between the Domestic Council and the White House. While Moynihan had allowed the cabinet secretaries who served as the subcommittee chairs to establish the agenda for their subcommittees and to assemble the staff from their departments, Ehrlichman had his staff set the subcommittee agendas and serve as staff for the subcommittees. While Moynihan had set broad parameters for the operations of the sub-committees, Ehrlichman set very specific parameters and reduced the options available for discussion.

However, the transition to the Domestic Council structure proved more difficult than Ehrlichman had envisioned. The domestic affairs staff in the White House, built from combining Moynihan's and Burns' staffs, had very different views on dealing with the departments and building plans of action. Moynihan's staff continued to allow the departments significant discretion and encouraged more liberal interpretations of policies than Burns' staff. According to Ehrlichman, the two staffs were like oil and water. "I inherited two absolutely diverse staffs," he said, "Moynihan's liberals and Burns' conservatives—and it was impossible to make it work or at least impossible for me to make it work. One by one I put people out to pasture."[69]

Ehrlichman Takes Control

Within a few months Ehrlichman had transferred nearly all of the Moynihan and Burns' staff to the departments or they had chosen to leave for non-

---

[67]Op. cit.

[68]The Rural Affairs Council was created on November 6, 1979, with Agriculture Secretary Clifford Hardin chairing the Council. The Council was designed to coordinate the administration's programs in rural affairs and to recommend policy initiatives to the president.

[69]Interview with John Ehrlichman in *Twenty-Two Intimate Perspectives of the Nixon Administration"*, edited by Kenneth Thompson, p 125.

government positions. The result was a domestic policy staff totally built by Ehrlichman with none of the vestiges of the failed Moynihan or Burns' operations. The cabinet-level Domestic Council was managed by Ehrlichman's staff. Its agenda, its meeting time and location (the Roosevelt Room), and its schedule were all set by the White House. The relative independence that the Urban Affairs Council subcommittees had been given disappeared with the new structure.

When the reorganization plan became official on July 1, 1970, the Urban Affairs Council ceased to exist (Figure 2.8). The executive order issued on July 1, 1970, "prescribing the duties of the Office of the Management and Budget and the Domestic Council" terminated the Council for Urban Affairs, the Cabinet Committee on the Environment, and the Council for Rural Affairs.[70] All three domestic advisory mechanisms had been added to the White House staff in 1969 to centralize policy development in the White House. But the design of each of the three units remained cabinet-based and often failed to provide initiatives that addressed Nixon's campaign promises or that protected his political interests. His decision to abandon these policy units in favor of the more centralized Domestic Council enabled him to move closer toward a domestic policy process that was more in line

- ◆ President
- ◆ Vice President
- ◆ Treasury
- ◆ Interior
- ◆ Agriculture
- ◆ Commerce
- ◆ Labor
- ◆ Health, Education and Welfare
- ◆ Housing and Urban Development
- ◆ Transportation
- ◆ Office of Economic Opportunity
- ◆ Postmaster General
- ◆ John Ehrlichman
- ◆ Robert Finch
- ◆ Bryce Harlow
- ◆ George Shultz
- ◆ Caspar Weinberger

Figure 2.8   Domestic Council,
                 July 1, 1970

[70]Council for Urban Affairs, created by executive order 11452 on January 23, 1969; Cabinet Committee on the Environment, created by executive order 11472 on May 29, 1969; Council for Rural Affairs, created by executive order 11493 on November 13, 1969.

man and Ehrlichman to ensure that the federal government pursue desegregation as required by the Supreme Court ruling. It was Ehrlichman's job to work with the departments to "do what the law requires—nothing more... On this subject a low profile is the key."[86] Elliot Richardson, who soon replaced Robert Finch at HEW, was directed by Nixon, with continual reinforcement from Ehrlichman, to minimize federal intervention in desegregation. "Do only what the law requires," was the White House refrain.

As Ehrlichman was focusing on civil rights and the day-to-day crises that emerged in the White House, one of his senior staff, John Whitaker, a Ph.D. in geology, was pursuing environmental issues. Whitaker was charged with managing the environmental issues, which polls indicated were a growing national concern. According to polls commissioned by the Domestic Council staff, 25% of the public said the environment was the most important political issue facing this country.[87] At Ehrlichman's direction, Whitaker was tapped to work on environmental strategies for the administration. Ehrlichman and Whitaker, who had begun his tenure on the White House as staff secretary, were involved in a host of major environmental initiatives, including establishment of the Environmental Protection Agency on December 2, 1970, and a major presidential message on the environment on January 22, 1970. Nixon proposed a $4 billion federal plan for construction of waste treatment plants, strengthening water pollution laws, and strengthening air pollution laws. Among the immediate successes of the 1970 initiatives were the Clean Air Amendments of 1970, which limited auto emissions from automobiles and set stringent air pollution standards for industry.

In addition, Ehrlichman's staff worked with the newly created Council on Environmental Quality in the Executive Office of the President to establish a series of executive orders that reduced water and air pollution at federal facilities.

One indication of the Domestic Council staff's influence in environmental policy making involved its influence in the creation of additional urban parks by the National Park Service. Whitaker created a plan to move additional funding into urban parks to address Nixon's pledge to "bring the parks to the people." Whitaker attributes Nixon's deep interest in urban parks to his own youthful poverty and inability to afford long trips to Yosemite and Yellowstone.[88]

By the end of 1971, Ehrlichman's Domestic Council staff was firmly in control of the domestic agenda. Departmental policy making was controlled by the Domestic Council's working groups. Ehrlichman had established a

---

[86]John Ehrlichman, *Witness to Power*, p 227.

[87]John Whitaker as discussant, *Richard Nixon: Politician, President, Administrator*, edited by Leon Friedman and William F. Levantrosser, p 200.

[88]John Whitaker as discussant, *Richard Nixon: Politician, President, Administrator*, edited by Leon Friedman and William F. Levantrosser, p 202.

long-range planning section under Edwin Harper that served to fulfill the third part of Roy Ash's reorganization plan.[89] The reorganization plan had originally included a planning unit, a domestic policy council, and a budgeting unit all under the umbrella of the Office of Executive Management. Crisis management and major issues, such as the Supreme Court nominations of G. Harrold Carswell and Clement Haynesworth, were managed directly by Ehrlichman. He had also, throughout his tenure in the White House, been a senior member of Nixon's political strategy group known as the Key Biscayne group. This group, which included Nixon, Agnew, Rogers Morton, John Mitchell, Robert Finch, Bryce Harlow, Harry Dent, Ehrlichman, and Haldeman focused on domestic issues that were politically volatile.[90]

Among the many issues that Ehrlichman became involved with was the plan to reorganize the cabinet, which was outlined in Nixon's 1971 State of the Union address. The plan called for reducing the 12 cabinet departments to eight. The departments of State, Treasury, Defense, and Justice would not be affected, but the remaining departments would be merged into four new departments: Human Resources, Community Development, Natural Resources, and Economic Development. Congress refused to allow the reorganization to move forward and Nixon pulled back from a major lobbying effort as the 1972 election edged closer.

By mid-1972, Ehrlichman had gained Nixon's total confidence as the overseer of the administration's domestic agenda. He had successfully kept, as Leonard Garment noted, the "home front tranquil while [Nixon focused on] large foreign policy strategies."[91] Ehrlichman began to ease out of the day-to-day operations of running the Domestic Council staff and to focus on special projects, such as the reorganization bill. Ken Cole, Ehrlichman's senior deputy, moved into overall management of the Domestic Council staff (Figure 2.10), leaving Ehrlichman to work on whatever issues arose that required Nixon's immediate attention. Cole was officially named Executive Director of the Domestic Council in December 1972, although Ehrlichman retained his title of Assistant to the President for Domestic Affairs.

By 1972 the war in Vietnam was winding down, allowing Nixon to turn his attentions to detente with the Soviet Union and the opening of relations with China. The spring of 1972 was consumed with Nixon's trip to Moscow for his first summit with Leonid Brezhnev and later with arms negotiations. While Nixon focused on international diplomacy, Ehrlichman continued to

[89]Harper, a Ph.D. in political science, had been Ehrlichman's liaison with the Bureau of the Budget.

[90]Memorandum for the President from Harry Dent, "Political Strategy Sessions," November 10, 1969, Box 8, White House Special Files, President's Handwriting Collection, Nixon Presidential Materials, College Park, Maryland.

[91]Interview with Leonard Garment in *Twenty-Two Intimate Perspectives of the Nixon Administration*, edited by Kenneth Thompson, p 104.

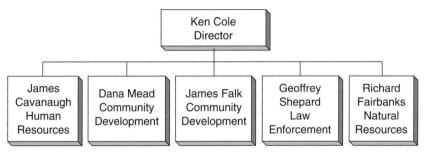

Figure 2.10   Domestic Council Senior Staff, 1972

oversee the domestic agenda at home. As the November election drew nearer, Ehrlichman began to direct more of his attentions to campaign issues and to delegate broader responsibility for domestic policy-making to Ken Cole.

The Second Term

The election of 1972 was a Nixon landslide victory over his Democratic opponent, George McGovern. Nixon received over 47 million votes, or 61% of the total, nearly 20 million more votes than McGovern. He had been given overwhelming support in his reelection bid, including the endorsement of 753 daily newspapers to the 56 that endorsed McGovern.

As Nixon entered his second term, he began to aggressively pursue a new domestic program, including a new welfare reform program, more programs to return power to state and local governments, and further reorganization of the cabinet. He had successfully visited Peking and Moscow, started nuclear arms negotiations in the Strategic Arms Limitation Talks (SALT), and reduced the United States ground forces in Vietnam from 550,000 to 20,000. The domestic agenda, for the first time in his presidency, was moving to the forefront of his attentions as the second term commenced. Nixon had scored major international accomplishments and was ready to turn to the homefront.

By 1973, Nixon had reframed the entire structure of the White House, centralizing both domestic and foreign policy operations in the Executive Office of the President. When Nixon took office, the budget for the Executive Office was $31 million; by 1973 that budget had nearly tripled to $71 million, providing for a staff of over 4000.[92] The White House staff was the largest in history, numbering 510 plus numerous other staff detailed from the agencies. The Domestic Council staff, which had grown as the White House

[92]Lou Cannon, "White House Staff—Nixon's Is Record in Size", *Washington Post*, January 7, 1973, p A1.

staff had, numbered nearly 80 and had become the unquestioned center of administration domestic policy making. Policies were focused by the White House and then programmatic details worked out in conjunction with the departments. A series of fourteen Domestic Council committees, which emerged from the Urban Affairs subcommittee structure, had been created to bring small groups of cabinet officers together to work on domestic policies (Figure 2.11). The structure of these committees was formed around the reorganization of the cabinet that Nixon proposed but never accomplished.[93] The committees were chaired by members of the cabinet, but the membership was a mix of cabinet members, Executive Office of the President staff (i.e., director of Office of Telecommunications Policy), White House staff (i.e., assistant to the president Baroody), and agency heads (i.e., director of the Civil Service Commission). Ehrlichman had carefully designed a struc-

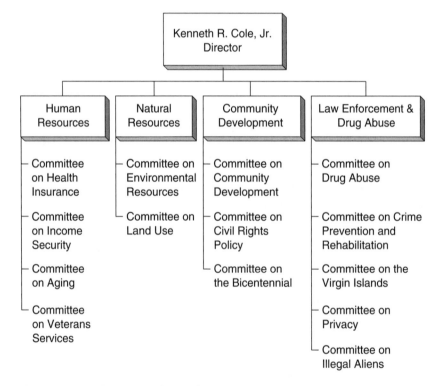

Figure 2.11   Domestic Council Committees, 1973–1974

[93]"The Domestic Council", Overview of Domestic Council developed by James Cannon for the 1976 transition, Box 21, James Cannon Transition Folder, December 1976, Gerald R. Ford Presidential Library, Ann Arbor, Michigan.

ture that ensured broad-based participation in policy development once the policy agenda was charted by the Domestic Council staff in cooperation with the larger White House staff (Figure 2.12). Participation in policy development by the departments, however, involved constant oversight by Ehrlichman's staff as the details were worked out.

Haldeman and Ehrlichman Resign

But the carefully designed structure that Ehrlichman created crumbled as Watergate began to dominate the president's daily life. The domestic agenda for the second term was eclipsed by the rising tide of the Watergate scandal and all but withered away as Ehrlichman and senior White House staff became deeply involved in plotting to keep the White House staff and the president from being implicated in the Watergate break-in, in which the Democratic headquarters in the Watergate complex had been broken-into in the middle of the night by burglars hired by the Committee to Re-Elect the President (CREEP).

Nearly everyone on the White House staff seemed to be embroiled in the events of the Watergate scandal. Nixon tried to avoid any connection to

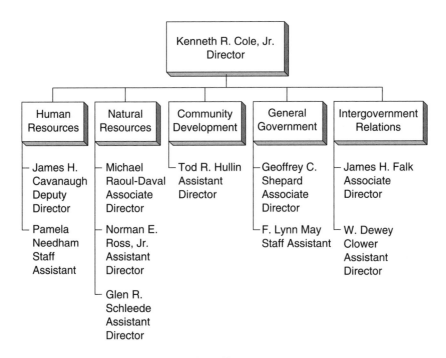

Figure 2.12   Domestic Council Staff, 1974

the break-in and repeatedly told the nation that he had not been involved in any of the Watergate activities. He blamed senior White House staff for wrong-doings. H. R. Haldeman and John Ehrlichman were subsequently implicated in the growing White House cover-up of the 1972 break-in. Haldeman and Ehrlichman were subsequently fired for their part in the Watergate coverup on April 30, 1973, and immediately left the White House.

Although he had left the White House, Watergate continued to dominate Ehrlichman's life. In 1975 John Ehrlichman was sent to federal prison for instigating unlawful acts during his White House years. He was accused of approving the 1971 break-in of Dr. Lewis Fielding's office by Howard Hunt and G. Gordon Liddy. Hunt and Liddy believed that Fielding, a psychiatrist, had files on Daniel Ellsberg, who had given the infamous Pentagon Papers to the *New York Times* at the height of the Vietnam War.

After Ehrlichman resigned from his White House position in 1973, Melvin Laird (Defense secretary from 1969 to 1973) was moved into the position of Assistant to the President for Domestic Affairs. Laird held the position for six months, from June, 1973, until January, 1974. However, little was moved forward during the Laird interregnum. Laird left in January, 1974, and Ken Cole was moved into the position of Assistant to the President for Domestic Affairs. However, as Watergate completely dominated the White House, neither Laird nor Cole had any significant chance of initiating new domestic policies or of overseeing the departments. All of the Domestic Council structures and committees remained intact, although they were rarely used as Watergate overshadowed every facet of White House decision-making. By the end of 1973, the departments rather than the White House had emerged as the center of domestic policy making. Cabinet officers began moving in their own directions without seeking White House approval or working in concert with other departments.

By the time Ken Cole took over as director, the Domestic Council was only a shadow of its former self. It was no longer the heart of domestic policy making. Rather, it had been relegated to a papermill: writing talking points for the president, preparing presidential messages, reviewing enrolled bills, and dealing with the daily White House crisis issues. Rather than an office for policy development, the Domestic Council had become an office for fire-fighting.

Richard Nixon ultimately resigned from the presidency in August, 1974, after acknowledging that he had participated in a cover-up of the Watergate break-in.

The Legacy in Domestic Affairs

Although the Nixon administration ended in disgrace, its legacy in domestic policy making remains. Richard Nixon was the first president to establish a

the need for a White House staff with "someone in charge of administration" and a continuation of the current structures for domestic policy, national security policy, economic policy, and the budget.[7]

Transition Team Reviews Domestic Policy Structure

The transition team firmly supported the Domestic Council's continuation in its present structure. This was a significant step in the life of the Domestic Council, because it was far from institutionalized in the White House and had lost a great deal of its authority in the last two years of the Nixon administration. However, the transition team recommended a change in the staff of the Domestic Council, essentially removing it from White House control. According to the report, the cabinet secretary would serve as executive director of the Domestic Council, rather than having a member of the president's personal staff serve as executive director of the Domestic Council, such as Ehrlichman and Cole had for Nixon.

The transition report provided for the cabinet secretary to "work with the cabinet and agency heads to provide program ideas, policy options, and recommendations needed for decisions on major domestic policy issues."[8] The purpose of changing the executive director of the Domestic Council staff from a member of the White House staff to a member of the cabinet was, according to the transition report, to allow "the Cabinet and other agency heads to be the principal spokesmen of the administration on policy issues, rather than OMB or White House staff."[9] The Nixon White House had left deep scars in the cabinet. Rather than an administration of cabinet government, as Nixon had promised, the cabinet had been ignored in their policy recommendations to the White House. The cabinet's frustration at being left out of the policy-making process after the first year of the Nixon administration was constantly repeated by different cabinet members as they spoke to members of the Rumsfeld transition team.

A Proposal on the Domestic Council

Their recommendation to Ford that domestic policy making be returned to the cabinet by removing the Domestic Council's staff from the White House was part of their plan to return to cabinet government. As Roger Porter noted in his evaluation of the Ford White House, "The basic thrust of the

[7]Transition Team Report to the President, August 20, 1974, by Rumsfeld, Marsh, Morton, and Scranton, Box 63, Buchen Transition Folder, Gerald R. Ford Presidential Library, Ann Arbor, Michigan.
[8]Transition Team Report to the President, August 20, 1974, by Rumsfeld, Marsh, Morton, Scranton, Box 63, Buchen Transition Folder, Gerald R. Ford Library, Ann Arbor, Michigan.
[9]Op cit.

transition team was clear: Rely much more heavily on cabinet departments and transfer the key chairmanships outside the White House."[10] The plan also met another criteria established by the transition team for open government. By moving the Domestic Council staff to a department, the administration was further opening its decision-making processes and providing greater access to decision makers. The specter of Watergate and the secretiveness that cloaked the White House in its final year was moving a step further away as Ford tried to open every facet of the White House decision-making structure.

The discussion on the Domestic Council staff was soon eclipsed by other debates in the White House. There is no evidence that Ken Cole, director of the Domestic Council staff, was aware of these discussions or that the discussions had moved further than the report presented to the president. If Cole was aware of any discussions on the Domestic Council, he made no move to counter them, perhaps realizing that his tenure was already limited by virtue of his being a Nixon holdover.

It appears that the transition report on the Domestic Council remained merely a report, for the Domestic Council continued to operate without any interruption or discussion with Cole. The most likely reason that the report faded away was that in-fighting among the staff overshadowed all other discussions in the White House for over a month. Al Haig, Nixon's chief of staff, and Robert Hartmann, Ford's vice presidential chief of staff, battled daily for control of Ford's schedule. Haig insisted that, as chief of staff, all memos to Ford be routed through him, which Hartmann and other vice presidential staff refused to agree to. Dick Cheney, who later joined the Ford White House staff, described the Haig-Hartmann feud in lively terms.

> An open feud between two of the White House staff developed. Hartmann was telling reporters that the emotionally spent Haig, who had shepherded Nixon through the final months, had to go quickly. Haig countered by implying that Hartmann drank too much.[11]

By mid-September, the lines had been drawn within the Ford White House with three distinct factions each battling for supremacy: the Nixon hold-overs led by Haig; the Hartmann team from the vice-president's office and the House; and an assortment of newly acquired staff.

Ford moved slowly to create a unified staff, largely out of consideration for the Nixon holdovers who needed to find new jobs. In an interview with A. James Reichley, Ford said, "I felt when I came into office that it would be wrong to clean out the Nixon appointees on a wholesale basis. Everyone, I

---

[10]Roger Porter, *The Economic Policy Board* (Cambridge, England: Cambridge University Press, 1980), p 37.

[11]Juan Cameron, "The Management Problem in Ford's White House," *Fortune,* July 1995, p 77.

felt, should have four or five months to give them a reasonable chance to find other jobs."[12] Ford generously gave all of the Nixon staff until January to find jobs.

The recommendation to create a unified staff, although slow in being implemented, had been made by the Buchen transition team. On the day that Ford took the oath of office, one of the memos in the fifty-page looseleaf binder, said, "You must walk a delicate line between compassion and consideration for the former President's staff and the rapid assertion of your personal control over the executive branch."[13] The memo concluded that the new president "short-term" the remaining Nixon White House staff.

By the end of September, Ford had finally removed Haig as chief of staff and, much to Hartmann's chagrin, named Donald Rumsfeld as "staff coordinator."[14] When Rumsfeld was introduced to the White House staff for the first time on September 24, Ford showed his frustration at the chaos that had overtaken the White House. He gathered the senior staff and said that he expected Rumsfeld to quickly design a staff structure that would provide "an orderly decision process" and end the petty rivalries that had dominated the White House.[15] Rumsfeld left his position at NATO and began his position in the White House on October 1, 1974.[16]

The Rumsfeld White House

As soon as Rumsfeld took over as the senior member of the White House staff, a new staffing arrangement emerged in which all senior White House staff had equal access to the president. The structure was often referred to as "the-spokes-of-the-wheel" structure, since all of the spokes revolved around the president. Ford described the new staff structure as more similar to the Johnson than the Nixon governing style:

> When I was in the House I observed how different Presidents seemed to organize the White House differently. President Nixon had had a very tightly held

[12]A. James Reichley, *Conservatives in An Age of Change*, p 293.

[13]Richard Reeves, *A Ford, Not a Lincoln*, p 72.

[14]Rumsfeld had been among several names on the list developed by Philip Buchen and T. R. Beal for the position of Chief of Administration. See Memo to Philip Buchen from T. R. Beal, September 20, 1974, Box 63, Buchen Transition Folder, Gerald R. Ford Presidential Library, Ann Arbor, Michigan.

[15]John Osborne, "White House Watch: Shakeout", *The New Republic*, October 26, 1974, p 9.

[16]Rumsfeld had been ambassador to the NATO since 1973; director of the Cost of Living Council 1972–73; Counsellor to the President 1971–72; director of the Office of Economic Opportunity 1969–71; Congressman from Illinois 1962–69. In 1965 Rumsfeld helped Ford oust Charles Halleck as Minority Leader in the House, a move that provided a lasting bond between the two.

organization with a chief of staff who ran the total operation. President Johnson seemed to have more intimate contact than President Nixon had with various people that reported from the defense and domestic side...When I became President...I initially felt that what I perceived as the Johnson organization was preferable, with seven or eight different people within the White House reporting directly to the president.[17]

The spokes-of-the-wheel system that Ford and Rumsfeld created involved eight senior staff. In a formal staff reorganization that became effective December 18, Rumsfeld announced the new Ford White House staff (Figure 3.1).

The titles and roles of each of these staff members, however, was essentially the same as they had been under Nixon. Rumsfeld, who constantly denied being a chief of staff, served in basically the same role that H. R. Haldeman had. Rumsfeld met with almost everyone that Ford did in the Oval Office and cleared most meetings that Ford had. Although senior staff and cabinet members had an easier time getting through to Ford, Rumsfeld inevitably would sit in on the meetings. Dick Cheney, who later joined the White House staff, gave this reasoning for Rumsfeld's participation in Oval Office meetings, particularly with cabinet members:

> Cabinet members, left to their own devices, want wide-open access to the president. They want to be able to walk and talk to him face to face about their problem and to get a decision from him and then implement it.[18]

But the logic was essentially the same for White House staff, who also wanted a quick decision from the president and the permission to implement that decision. Rumsfeld saw his role as providing time for the president to "get a broader perspective," as Cheney noted.

- ◆ Donald Rumsfeld—Assistant to the President
- ◆ Robert Hartmann—Counsellor to the President
- ◆ Philip Buchen—Counsel to the President
- ◆ John Marsh—Counsellor to the President
- ◆ Henry Kissinger—National Security Adviser
- ◆ William Seidman—Economic Affairs
- ◆ Ron Nessen—Press Secretary
- ◆ Ken Cole—Domestic Policy Adviser

Figure 3.1   White House Staff,
December 18, 1974

[17]A. James Reichley, *A Discussion with Gerald Ford* (Washington, D.C.: American Enterprise Institute, 1977), p 4.
[18]Interview with Dick Cheney, *The Ford Presidency: Twenty-Two Intimate Perspectives of Gerald R. Ford,* Kenneth Thompson, editor, (Lanham, Maryland: University Press of America, 1988), p 68–69.

The White House staff structure that Rumsfeld developed provided broad access to Ford for both the cabinet and the White House staff to ensure the perception of an open presidency. The transition team's recommendation that Ford's first priority should be rebuilding public confidence in the president and the office of the presidency became the guiding principle in organizing the White House. The White House staff's open access to the president would become a symbol of Ford's commitment to open government.

The December 18, 1974, staff reorganization announcement also provided a statement on the role that the White House staff would play in its interactions with the departments. Their role would be limited "to those that must necessarily be performed within the White House." The cabinet and agency heads would be relied on to perform all appropriate functions best performed by their organizations, according to the reorganization plan. While this relationship between the cabinet and the White House staff supported Ford's decision to reduce the power of the White House staff and enhance cabinet access to the Oval Office, it also appeared to reduce the role of the White House staff in policy making. Rumsfeld's view of the White House staff would later prove to be considerably different from Rockefeller's view of the role that the Domestic Council staff should play.

The Domestic Policy Process

At the same time in which Ford was working on his White House staff structure, he was also reviewing the policy-making units within the White House. The two primary policy-making units, the National Security Council and the Domestic Council, were kept intact. Except for the brief discussion during the transition that concerned moving the executive director of the Domestic Council to the cabinet, no significant discussions were held on either the National Security Council or the Domestic Council.

The primary discussion on policy making involved creation of a separate unit for managing economic policy. Under Nixon, the assistant to the president for domestic affairs and the Domestic Council staff had coordinated domestic policy, which often included decisions on economic policy issues. Major economic policy issues during the Nixon administration were handled by the economic team composed of the secretary of the Treasury, chairman of the Council of Economic Advisers, and the director of the Office of Management and Budget (often referred to as the troika). At the end of his second term, Nixon appointed Kenneth Rush to the White House staff as counsellor to the president for economic affairs to manage the rising problems of inflation. However, Rush was given little authority and was, as the rest of the White House staff, rendered essentially powerless by Watergate.

Soon after taking office, William Seidman, an investment banker who had been working on Ford's vice presidential staff, convinced Ford to consider creating a separate unit in the White House to manage economic policy. Seidman and Rush presented a package to Ford that proposed the Economic Policy Board. Under the Seidman-Rush scenario, the Economic Policy Board would become the third unit in the White House to manage a policy area. The Economic Policy Board would become the equivalent of the Domestic Council and the National Security Council within the White House organization. After considerable debate among the White House senior staff, Ford agreed to the Seidman-Rush proposal. On September 30, 1974, Ford signed executive order #11808 creating the Economic Policy Board (EPB), the third major policy unit in the White House.

Creation of the Economic Policy Board was intended to provide Ford greater help in dealing with the severe economic problems that he had inherited from Nixon. Inflation and unemployment were both rising, leading Ford to declare in his first address to Congress that "Inflation was Public Enemy Number One." For Ford, the most important policy decisions at the start of his administration involved turning the economy around. The Economic Policy Board provided a mechanism to focus all of the administration's resources on the one issue that Ford wanted to deal with immediately: the economy.

While Ford's attention was directed to the creation of the Economic Policy Board, the Domestic Council continued to operate during the fall of 1974 in the same capacity it had under Nixon following the downfall of John Ehrlichman: preparing presidential messages, reviewing enrolled bills, developing options papers for departmental proposals, and handling daily crisis management in domestic affairs (Figure 3.2). Under Ken Cole, the Domestic Council played a low-key role in the White House during the early months of Ford's administration and was given little encouragement by Rumsfeld or Ford to return to its role as policy manager.

Cole rarely saw Ford and was kept out of key decisions by Rumsfeld.[19] Cole tried in September to have Ford provide direction for the Domestic Council, and he wrote a detailed memo outlining the types of activities in which the Domestic Council staff was involved.[20] But Ford never responded. In late October, Cole again sent Ford a memo outlining what he saw as the best course for the Council. He recommended that the Council be strengthened, with the "capacity for development of a think tank to generate new ideas." Cole went on to say that the Domestic Council had been unable to tackle the long-term planning that the Ash Council envisioned because of a lack of staff and the day-to-day assignments that had consumed its time.[21]

[19]"Rocky and Rummy: Getting Organized," *Time*, December 30, 1974, p 7.
[20]Memo from Ken Cole to Gerald Ford, September 10, 1974, Box 69, Domestic Council Organization Folder, James Cannon Files, Gerald R. Ford Presidential Library, Ann Arbor, Michigan.
[21]Memo from Ken Cole to Gerald Ford, October 25, 1974, Box 58, National Goals Research Staff Folder, Gerald R. Ford Presidential Library, Ann Arbor, Michigan.

Refusing to be deterred, Rockefeller continued to seek additional staff from Ford to handle long-range planning activities. In a formal request, Cannon wrote to Ford on July 16, 1975, about the futility of trying to handle both firefighting and long-range planning. Cannon sought to add an additional twenty-three professional staff and six secretarial staff. Ford agreed but the Senate again refused to appropriate the additional funds.

Only days after Cannon wrote to Ford seeking additional funding, Rockefeller received a memo from Ford on July 24 requesting that an extensive domestic policy review be undertaken. Ford saw these reviews serving as the basis for discussion papers to be circulated among White House staff on priorities that the 1976 State of the Union speech would address. Cannon immediately set up a new task force called the Domestic Council Review Group on Domestic Policy.

With a renewed sense of purpose, the Domestic Council staff began working with the departments through the new task force to forge a series of domestic priorities. They recommended that the process be opened up to include citizen input into prioritizing the domestic agenda, and Ford approved a series of six Public Forums on Domestic Policy. These would be one-day meetings to be held in Denver, Kansas City, Austin, Philadelphia, Nashville, and Los Angeles beginning October 21 and ending on December 9 1975.

But just as the Domestic Council staff was sensing a renewed role in shaping the domestic agenda, Ford pulled the rug out from under them. On October 6, 1975, Ford announced his proposal for the 1977 federal budget. "I propose," he said, "we halt the alarming growth in federal spending by holding spending in the coming year to $395 billion. That means a cut of $28 billion below what we will spend if we just stand still." He continued by proposing that federal spending be held below projected levels, essentially killing any chance for new domestic programs to be launched. Neither Rockefeller nor Cannon had been included in the decision to reduce spending and had not been forewarned about the announcement. Ford made the decision after consulting with Rumsfeld, OMB director James Lynn, and CEA chair Alan Greenspan.[41] The Domestic Forums suddenly became a moot operation that would have no significant effect on proposals in the State of the Union address. The budget announcement completely demoralized the Domestic Council staff. But the staff was already dealing with internal problems. As short-handed as the staff was, they often felt as if they were serving two masters: Ford and Rockefeller. Memos on departmental policy recommendations often had to be written twice—once for Ford and once for Rockefeller. Ford,

[41]Michael Nelson, "Rockefeller and the American Vice Presidency," *Gerald R. Ford and the Politics of Post-Watergate America, Volume 1,* edited by Bernard J. Firestone and Alexej Ugrinsky, p 150.

as Nixon had, wanted the decision memoranda that served as the cover memo on departmental policy issues, to provide a recommendation to be accepted or rejected. The recommendation had a box at the bottom from which the president could choose accept or not accept. If the president did not accept the recommendation, both Nixon and Ford would write a short note directing another course of action to be pursued.

Rockefeller wanted another structure used for memos on departmental policy recommendations. That structure involved a cover memo that gave the department's recommendation and then the Domestic Council staff recommendation. Rockefeller did not want the Domestic Council staff to make the final recommendation, but rather he wanted to choose from the various options and prepare a recommendation for Ford.[42]

The Domestic Council staff was also battling problems with the larger White House staff, whose loyalty was to Rumsfeld and Cheney, and they often tried to cut Cannon's staff out of the policy loop. According to John Casserly, a White House speechwriter, the White House was full of "arguing, backstabbing and quibbling."[43] The problem erupted even further when the Domestic Council staff received reports that Rumsfeld had been complaining about Rockefeller's activities at the Domestic Council to a group of Republican party leaders. Among other complaints that Rumsfeld had of Rockefeller was that he was too old to handle the grueling demands of the White House.[44] But Rockefeller, who was equally disdainful of Rumsfeld, viewed the White House staff as disorganized with few goals or principles for which they stood.[45]

Rockefeller Withdraws

After less than a year at the helm of the Domestic Council, Rockefeller realized that Ford did not intend to use the Domestic Council staff to develop major policy proposals. Whether he intended for Rockefeller to reshape the Domestic Council when the offer of the vice presidency was tendered and was convinced otherwise by Rumsfeld is not clear. The most likely answer is that Ford originally did intend to give Rockefeller broad discretion in domestic policy making but was later convinced by Rumsfeld and Cheney that, in order to control the deficit, the federal government would have to reduce spending. This position was also in line with that of conservative Republican leaders whose support Ford needed to regain the 1976 nomina-

[42]Interview with Richard Dunham, *Gerald R. Ford and the Politics of Post-Watergate America, Volume 1*, edited by Bernard J. Firestone and Alexej Ugrinsky, p 186.

[43]John J. Casserly, *The Ford White House* (Boulder, Colorado: Colorado Associate University Press, 1977), p 177.

[44]Ibid, p 177.

[45]Ibid, p 229.

tion. To stray from that position would be to risk losing their support to the rising challenge of California governor, Ronald Reagan.

On November 3, 1975, Rockefeller announced that he would not be Ford's running mate on the 1976 ticket. On December 16, 1975, nearly one year to the day after being confirmed as vice president, Rockefeller announced his resignation as vice chairman of the Domestic Council. In a searing memo to Ford, Rockefeller criticized the president for his failure to support a broader role for the Domestic Council than firefighting activities and for his failure to provide increased staffing. He also criticized Ford's failure to give one organizational unit, preferably the Domestic Council, authority to manage the domestic policy process. Under the current system, Rockefeller argued, the Economic Policy Board, the Office of Management and Budget, the Energy Resources Council, and the Council of Economic Advisers all provided advice on domestic policy making. Rockefeller noted that this advice was often without coordination or without any effort to view the long-term implications of decisions. In his concluding paragraphs, he lashed out at Rumsfeld and Cheney whom he accused of a constant failure to support the Domestic Council staff.[46]

The Domestic Council without Rockefeller

With Rockefeller gone, the Domestic Council staff quickly returned to the same role it had held under Ken Cole—firefighter.[47] The Ford White House staff (Rumsfeld, Cheney, Simon, and Seidman) closed ranks and shut out every vestige of the Rockefeller group in a policy-making role. James Cavanaugh, Rumsfeld's eyes and ears in the Domestic Council, was elevated to deputy assistant to the president for domestic affairs in addition to his role as deputy director of the Domestic Council. The Domestic Council staff became a reactive group after Rockefeller left, reacting to the daily crises that faced the White House. Rockefeller's plan for a proactive, involved Domestic Council staff was buried.

Cannon reorganized the Domestic Council staff in January, 1976, with a larger focus on operations. James Cavanaugh continued in the dual role of

[46]Memo From Nelson Rockefeller to Gerald Ford, December 16, 1975, Domestic Council Organization Folder, Box 64, James Cannon Files, Gerald R. Ford Presidential Library, Ann Arbor, Michigan.

[47]In an interview with Glen Schleede, an associate director of the Domestic Council, the question was posed: Is it fair to say that fighting fires consumes most of the time of most of the associate directors, handling the day-to-day problems that come up on the policy area of your particular subject area? Schleede responded, "That's a fair statement." See the oral history interview of Glenó R. Schleede by Stephen J. Wayne, May 1, 1976, Gerald R. Ford Presidential Library, Ann Arbor, Michigan.

deputy director of operations in addition to his new role in the White House.[48] Arthur Quern was named deputy director, replacing Richard Dunham, who had resigned in September, 1975. Quern, as had Dunham, would manage the small, long-range planning role of the staff. Cannon increased the intergovernmental affairs unit on the staff from three to five members, in line with Ford's push for greater avenues toward federalism.

In addition to the staff changes that Cannon made, Ford resurrected Daniel Patrick Moynihan's title of assistant to the president for urban affairs and added Arthur Fletcher as deputy assistant to the president for urban affairs (although he did not name an assistant to the president for urban affairs). Fletcher, who was black, was added to the staff to work with Cannon on urban problems and given the added title of deputy director of the Domestic Council. This, of course, added insult to injury for Rockefeller, for many of the issues that Rockefeller wanted to tackle involved inner-city initiatives. These ideas were generally ignored by Ford as too costly and out of line with Ford's proposals to shift policy making back to the state and local governments. Fletcher's appointment was announced only weeks after Rockefeller's departure.

But the Domestic Council staff continued to feel that it had little direction and little coordination with Rumsfeld and the other members of the White House staff. The staff meeting notes of January 21, 1976, of the Domestic Council reflected a sense of frustration among the staff. The council's secretary recorded that "there was much discussion of the lack of coordination between Domestic Council and Baroody's operations; Domestic Council and the Scheduling Operation; Domestic Council and the Press operation. JMC [Cannon] asked Cavanaugh to work with the White House staff and to try and get this untangled."[49] The reference to the "White House staff" is particularly striking, because it indicates that the Domestic Council staff felt alienated from other parts of the White House and did not consider themselves members of the White House staff.

Dick Cheney, who had taken over as staff coordinator following Donald Rumsfeld's appointment as secretary of defense, was reluctant to try to improve the working relationship between the Domestic Council staff and the larger White House staff. "I don't know any way to clean it up," Cheney said.[50]

---

[48]Cavanaugh's appointment to the White House staff was made to allow him to participate in election activities. As a member of the Domestic Council staff he was prevented by the Hatch Act from engaging in any partisan projects. The dual appointment provided Cavanaugh White House status and thus exempted him from the Hatch Act.

[49]Staff Meeting Minutes, January 21, 1976, Domestic Council Staff Meeting (2) Folder, Box 14, James Cannon files, Gerald R. Ford Library, Ann Arbor, Michigan.

[50]Interview with Dick Cheney, *The Ford Presidency: Twenty-Two Intimate Perspectives of Gerald R. Ford,* edited by Kenneth W. Thompson, p 66–67.

Cannon's decision to use the Domestic Council staff to handle day-to-day policy-management problems reflected his own view that Ford never really intended for Rockefeller to move the Domestic Council into a proactive role. "What President Ford wanted the Domestic Council to do was essentially to deal with putting out brush fires, to move paper back and forth between the departments and the White House."[51]

Perhaps Cannon understood Ford more clearly than Rockefeller did since he regularly attended senior staff meetings and participated in the wide-ranging discussions on Ford's policy agenda. Rockefeller was told by Ford in August, 1974, that he wanted Rockefeller to turn the Domestic Council into the domestic equivalent of the National Security Council. That pledge was reaffirmed on February 13, 1974, when Ford outlined the broad responsibilities in domestic policy making that he was giving Rockefeller. With these mandates, Rockefeller moved forward.

Cannon, however, was part of the day-to-day operations of the White House and quickly realized that Rumsfeld was moving Ford toward a more conservative approach to policy making that precluded any new domestic initiatives. It became eminently clear to Cannon that Ford was not going to revamp the Domestic Council and, in fact, wanted to continue its role as a firefighting unit. Rockefeller, who was not part of the daily operations of the White House, never understood that Ford was backing away from his plans to develop domestic initiatives and was focusing all of his efforts on economic issues. When Rockefeller left, Cannon refocused the Domestic Council staff in a direction more in tune with the broader White House staff.

Focusing on Brushfires

The brief resurrection of the Domestic Council staff as a policy maker lasted only ten months. However, in its brief life it had been involved with a wide array of policy initiatives: national health insurance, the bailout of New York City and programs to prevent urban insolvency, predator control, an energy plan (the Energy Independence Authority), programs for drug abuse prevention, and urban mass-transit aid. Rockefeller had clearly given new life to the Domestic Council and returned it to the role that the Ash Council had envisioned. But ultimately, the role that Roy Ash and Nelson Rockefeller envisioned for the Domestic Council proved quite different from the one that Gerald Ford envisioned. By the end of the Ford administration, the Domestic Council staff was focusing on brushfires. As Gerald Ford noted in his memoirs, the primary function of his administration had not been agenda-setting

[51]John Robert Greene, *The Presidency of Gerald Ford*, (Lawrence, Kansas: University Press of Kansas, 1995) p 84.

but providing the nation a time to heal. He believed that he had accomplished what he set out to: restoring the confidence and trust of the American people in their political leadership, institutions, and processes. This had been the primary objective established by the transition team for the new administration and that objective had been very successfully accomplished.

THE CARTER PRESIDENCY:
FOCUS ON GOVERNMENT EFFICIENCY

With the resignation of Richard Nixon in August, 1974, Gerald Ford had become the nation's first unelected president. His brief two-and-a-half year tenure had focused less on policy initiation than on restoring dignity and trust to the presidency. Ford had been successful at rebuilding confidence in the presidency itself but less successful at rebuilding support for his own presidency, due largely to his pardon of Richard Nixon. The pardon, issued on Sunday morning, September 8, 1974, had been based on Ford's deep conviction that Nixon could not receive a fair trial by jury.[1] His view, however noble, was shared by few Americans. Although Ford saw the pardon as an opportunity to close the chapter on Watergate,[2] the public viewed the pardon quite differently. For many, the pardon was yet another failure in presidential leadership. The door was then easily opened for a challenge by the Democrats for the oval office, a challenge mounted by James Earl Carter, Jr., the former governor of Georgia who captured the Democratic nomination for president in 1976.[3]

Carter's candidacy capitalized on the nation's frustration at the Nixon pardon, on Watergate, and on the Ford administration's failure to move forward with a proactive domestic agenda. As he began his formal campaign, Carter said, "Our nation is drifting without purpose...it is time to get our country on the move again."[4] Carter's theme throughout the campaign was

---

[1]Gerald R. Ford, *A Time To Heal* (New York: Harper and Row, 1979), p 177.
[2]Op cit.
[3]Carter served as governor of Georgia from 1971–1975. He spent the next two years actively pursuing the Democratic presidential nomination. For a detailed discussion of Carter's primary battles, see Charles O. Jones, *The Trustee Presidency: Jimmy Carter and the United States Congress* (Baton Rouge, Louisiana: Louisiana State University Press, 1988).
[4]Gordon A. Haas, *Jimmy Carter and Politics of Frustration* (Jefferson, North Carolina: McFarland & Company, Inc., 1992), p 43. The campaign kick-off on September 6, 1976, from Warm Springs, Georgia, the summer retreat of Franklin Delano Roosevelt, was intended to tie the presidential campaign of Jimmy Carter with the successful presidency of Roosevelt.

that the American people had lost faith in a government that had lied to its citizens, a government that covered up its own mistakes, and an administration that allowed these offenses to go unpunished. Carter repeatedly, and ultimately successfully, tied Gerald Ford to the Nixon administration and its complicity in the Watergate events. Carter called for an "open administration that could prevent the recurrence of Watergate."[5] It was time, according to Carter, to reform government to ensure that it was "honest and competent, with clear purpose and strong leadership."[6]

The 1976 campaign was one of few substantive issues. The specter of Watergate dominated the campaign, and Carter used every means available to keep the issue at the forefront of his speeches and public appearances. In a speech delivered on June 1, 1976, at the dedication of a new wing of the Martin Luther King Hospital in Los Angeles, Carter built on Martin Luther King's famous "I have a dream" speech and scathingly attacked the Nixon/Ford years. "I see an American government," he said, "that has turned away from scandals and corruption and official cynicism and finally become as decent as our people... I see an American government that does not spy on its citizens or harass its citizens, but respects your dignity and your privacy and your right to be let alone. This is the America that I see."[7]

Ford was clearly vulnerable to the constant reminders of Watergate by the Democratic challenger. Carter used such nonconcrete themes as "doing what is right" for the nation and the need for new leaders and "a time of healing." He frequently described the central theme of the campaign as "the desire of the American people to have faith again in our government, to [have] a fresh start,"[8] and peppered his campaign speeches with words such as *honesty, sensitivity, hope, love, patriotism,* and *pride.* The Carter campaign never failed to tie Ford to Nixon and to remind the nation of Watergate.

Carter's strategy was to capitalize on the nation's anathema toward Washington that stemmed from Watergate and to campaign as a "Washington outsider." After carefully linking Ford to Nixon and the insidious nature of insider politics, Carter billed himself as an outsider saying, "A lot of us are outsiders. We don't see why these strange things happen in Washington."[9] His slogan became "A Leader for a Change."

[5]Neal Peirce, "The Democratic Nominee...If I Were President," *National Journal,* July 17, 1976, p 991.

[6]Erwin C. Hargrove, *Jimmy Carter as President: Leadership and the Politics of the Public Good* (Baton Rouge, Louisiana: Louisiana State University Press, 1988), p 12.

[7]Patrick Anderson, *Electing Jimmy Carter: The Campaign of 1976* (Baton Rouge, Louisiana: Louisiana State University Press, 1994), p 175.

[8]Kandy Stroud, *How Jimmy Won* (New York: William Morrow and Company, Inc., 1977), p 342.

[9]Gordon A. Haas, *Jimmy Carter and the Politics of Frustration,* p 42.

Campaign 1976: Setting the Domestic Agenda

While Carter's campaign tied Ford to Nixon and Watergate and focused on the need for an outsider in the White House, it was not without its share of routine campaign rhetoric promising to improve the economy and rebuild fractured relations with Congress. Carter went on the attack, criticizing the Ford administration's record in domestic policy. "It is a record," he said, "I cite more in sorrow than in anger, for it is a record of political insensitivity, of missed opportunities, of constant conflict with Congress, and of national neglect."[10] Carter's preference for campaigning against Ford's record and the Republican Party in general, rather than campaigning for his own agenda, was repeated throughout the campaign. "This campaign has been joined a hundred times over," he said, "whenever our party has fought for legislation that would benefit the average American—for Social Security, for minimum wage laws, for rural electrification, for voting rights, for Medicare—and our opponent's party has fought against all that progress."[11]

Once Carter had set the framework for attacking the Ford administration's absence of domestic initiatives and its veto of Congressionally supported domestic programs, the Carter campaign staff, led by Stuart Eizenstat, assembled a broad, nonspecific set of policy positions. Those positions included pledges to reduce joblessness, establish a national health insurance system, and reform the welfare program. Although deficit reduction was not the focal point of the campaign as it would become nearly twenty years later when Bill Clinton sought the presidency, Carter vowed to balance the federal budget by the end of his four-year term. The deficit in 1976 was about $50 billion; however, his plans for balancing the budget were vague and offered no specific plans for cutting programs.

In large part, Carter proposed to balance the budget and reduce federal spending through reorganizing the federal government. "The present bureaucratic structure of the federal government is a mess," Carter said during his first debate with Ford. Carter proposed to reestablish the authority granted by Congress under the 1939 Reorganization Act that allowed the president to reorganize the executive branch, subject to Congressional veto. That authority had lapsed in 1973, as Congress sought to curb Richard Nixon's powers.

Reducing federal spending could also be accomplished, according to Carter, by simply improving departmental procedures for budgeting. "Programs will not be allowed to proceed," Carter said, "until they have satisfactorily demonstrated that they accomplish a valid and feasible objective, at a

[10]Kandy Stroud, *How Jimmy Won*, p 342–43.
[11]Patrick Anderson, *Electing Jimmy Carter: The Campaign of 1976*, p 107.

reasonable and affordable cost, in furtherance of the priorities of the nation and the needs of the people."[12] Carter proposed a detailed review of every federal program annually to determine whether there was duplication or overlapping of services.

Eizenstat promised that, once elected, Carter would provide a detailed plan to review programs and to reorganize the federal government. Although Carter could not, Eizenstat argued, prepare such a detailed plan in the short span of the campaign, he could prepare a proposal that exemplified reorganization. On September 21, 1976, Carter issued his energy reorganization plan, a plan that was described as an example of the overall reorganization scheme. Under the energy reorganization plan, Carter proposed creation of a Department of Energy, which would consolidate programs spread among twenty departments and agencies. The consolidation would result in the abolition of the Federal Energy Administration, the Energy Research and Development Administration, and the Federal Power Commission. Carter similarly called for creation of a Department of Education, that would consolidate education programs, and a revamping of health programs into one department.

Such emphasis on federal reorganization exemplified the overall campaign theme that Washington needed an "outsider." By campaigning against the entrenched bureaucracy and its proliferation of programs, Carter had emphasized Ford's contribution to a dysfunctional government. Carter needed only to promise "new leadership," he believed, to build public support for his promise of government efficiency.

Addressing Limited Domestic Issues

While a balanced budget, efficiency in government, and reorganization were the keystones of the campaign, Carter did address a limited number of domestic issues. Chief among those issues was the economy and a promise to reduce the unemployment rate to 4% and to simultaneously reduce inflation to 4% by the end of his first term. Carter argued for more private investment but also for increased numbers of public sector jobs. He offered few specifics except to urge an expansionary fiscal and monetary policy to stimulate demand, production, and jobs.

His domestic agenda was generally confined to four areas: energy, the environment, national health care, and welfare reform. In energy, he wanted not only the creation of a federal energy department, but a stronger federal presence in energy management. In particular, Carter wanted to encourage energy conservation and to seek alternative sources of energy in order to

---

[12]Joel Havemann, "Carter's Long Journey Ends in Victory on a Long Night," *National Journal,* November 6, 1976, p 1587.

reduce dependence on foreign oil supplies. Carter was concerned that instability in the Middle East could seriously disrupt U.S. oil supplies and lead to massive shortages around the nation.

His environmental goals were largely tied to his energy goals, which he saw as intertwined. He wanted to ensure cleaner air and tied cleaner air to mandates for stronger auto emission pollution standards. He sought alternative energy sources and wanted coal to be reduced where strip mining had destroyed the landscape. He wanted to increase U.S. oil reserves and wanted to protect the oceans from oil rig disasters. For Carter, improving the nation's energy resources was interdependent with managing the environment.

The other two issues on which the Carter campaign focused were comprehensive national health care and restructuring the welfare program. Few specifics were given for either. Typical of the vague statements on these two issues was a statement by Carter at an August 16 press briefing. "Welfare laws, which are now multitudinous and sometimes overlapping and wasteful and very confusing, ought to be greatly simplified."[13] The central theme of the campaign, however, remained the attack on Gerald Ford and his ties to the Nixon administration and the reorganization of the federal government. The domestic agenda was a secondary focus.

The Transition

When the voters spoke on November 2, 1976, they rejected a continuation of the Ford presidency. Jimmy Carter, who had shed his more formal name of James Earl Carter, Jr., captured the White House by more than a million votes. Carter's popular vote edge was 40,828,929 (51%) to Ford's 38,148,940 (48%), and his electoral edge was 297 to 241. Third party candidate Eugene McCarthy garnered 1% of the popular vote. Although it was not a stunning victory or a landslide, it remained a clear mandate for Carter. Gerald Ford, who had gained the office by appointment, had not been able to gain it by election.

More so than any previous president-elect, Jimmy Carter had prepared for the transition of power. Following the Pennsylvania primary election in April, 1976, Carter set in motion an informal transition team in Atlanta, under the direction of Jack Watson. According to Watson, the purpose of the early transition team work was to "talk quietly and gather information quietly so that by the time we were required to put options in front of the president we could do so with some degree of confidence, that the options . . . were well considered."[14] The transition team, true to Watson's promise, was rarely in the public eye and maintained an exceedingly low profile.

[13]Ibid, p. 1587.
[14]Interview with Jack Watson.

Transition Teams

Once Carter was elected, however, Watson moved to the high profile position of transition director and moved his office from Atlanta to Washington, D.C. He expanded the transition operation to examine not only the transfer of power but key issues that immediately would face the new administration. This involved bringing on board a sizeable group of 132 paid staffers to work on the policy issues and personnel hirings for the administration. Stuart Eizenstat, issues coordinator during the campaign, became the transition coordinator of the office of policy analysis and agency liaison, including both domestic and foreign policy areas. Hamilton Jordan, Carter's campaign manager, became coordinator of the "personnel advisory group," which concentrated on White House staff and cabinet positions, and Matthew Coffee, president of the Association of Radio Stations, managed the search for the remaining senior departmental positions. Coffee directed the talent inventory program, which Watson had developed during the campaign, to collect and sort names for the new administration.[15] Nearly 30,000 job seekers sent resumes to the Talent Inventory Program, of which 10,000 were selected and listed as possibilities for senior positions of assistant secretary or above.[16]

Jordan and Coffee: Personnel Management

The talent inventory program had not only developed a sophisticated listing of names that met the needs of various departments but had included women and minorities in the lists. Carter demanded of his cabinet nominees that they actively recruit women and minorities, telling them to "canvass both the number and the type of openings in the agency. The initial commitment must be to place a substantial number of women and minorities in nontraditional jobs and not restrict them to positions they have traditionally held." He further stated that "The Talent Inventory Program in the Transition Office has assembled resumes of scores of minorities and females who are both qualified for and interested in serving at the Assistant or Deputy Assistant Secretary Level."[17] Although Carter encouraged diversifying the departmental ranks, he did not require it nor did he institute a quota system. He allowed cabinet secretaries discretion in hiring and simply asked, "As soon as

[15]Bruce Adams and Kathryn Kavanaugh-Baran, *Promise and Performance: Carter Builds a New Administration* (Lexington, Massachusetts: Lexington Books, 1979), p 12.
[16]Joel Havemann, "The TIP Talent Hunt—Carter's Original Amateur Hour," *National Journal*, February 2, 1977, p 268.
[17]Memo from Jimmy Carter to Cabinet Designees, "Appointment of Women and Minority Males to High Level Positions," December 22, 1976, Carter-Mondale Transition Group, Box FG-96, Hamilton Jordan Files, Jimmy Carter Presidential Library, Atlanta, Georgia.

you have settled on an individual for a particular position, notify Hamilton Jordan in writing."[18] Jordan's primary responsibility was to develop a selection process for White House staff and cabinet officers, plus senior administration staff.

Watson and Eizenstat: Policy Management

While Jordan and Coffee were overseeing the personnel management phase of the transition, Watson and Eizenstat were overseeing the policy management phase of the transition. Their focus was particularly on reviewing legislation and treaties that would expire in 1977 and on reestablishing reorganization authority for the new president. Carter's campaign pledge to move toward a rapid reorganization of the federal government was premised on Congressional approval of reorganization authority. If the administration were to "hit the ground running," reorganization authority had to be shepherded through Congress with few delays.

Reorganization Examined

The Watson/Eizenstat team jumped quickly into action reviewing reorganization authority and developed reorganization plans that included cutting the number of federal agencies from their existing level of 1900 to a proposed level of 200. The changes would involve not only restructuring existing agencies but abolishing nearly 1400 federal advisory committees.

While part of the team was focusing on reorganization of the federal government, another part was focusing on reorganization of the White House. Watson wanted to create a White House staff structure that reflected Carter's fluid operating style, noting that, "One of the clearest lessons is that the White House staff organization is the personal reflection of the president and what will work beautifully for one President may not work at all for the next President."[19]

The staff structure that Watson pursued was a spokes-of-the-wheel structure, without a chief of staff, with several senior staff having direct access to the president (Figure 4.1). Jody Powell, Carter's spokesman, said in a press conference soon after the election that it was "not [Carter's] intention to have a single chief of staff. He believes in having a number of people with

---

[18]Memo from The President to Members of the Cabinet, "Procedures Regarding Appointments in Your Department," February 8, 1977, Box FG 96, Hamilton Jordan Files, Jimmy Carter Presidential Library, Atlanta, Georgia.
[19]Dom Bonafede, "Carter Staff Is Getting Itchy To Move to Washington," *National Journal*, October 30, 1976, p 1544.

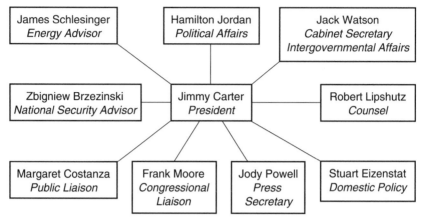

Figure 4.1　White House Senior Staff

relatively equal access. It is the way he operated the governor's office in Georgia ... and the way we operated the campaign."[20]

Cabinet members would have direct access to the president, in line with Carter's support for cabinet government. Carter wanted a White House staff structure that provided for "openness" in the decision-making process by allowing a wide variety of people direct access to the president. Watson repeatedly emphasized that Carter did not want a chief of staff who controlled access to the Oval Office but wanted open access to the Oval Office by senior staff and cabinet members. The spokes-of-the-wheel structure that emerged included nine senior staff with direct access to Carter:

1. Hamilton Jordan, Political Affairs[21]
2. Jack Watson, Cabinet Secretary and Intergovernmental Affairs[22]
3. Robert Lipshutz, Counsel
4. Stuart Eizenstat, Domestic Policy
5. Jody Powell, Press Secretary[23]
6. Frank Moore, Congressional Liaison
7. Margaret Costanza, Public Liaison

[20]Edward Walsh, "Carter Reviewing Memo on Selecting Top Aides," *Washington Post*, November 10, 1976, p A16.

[21]Hamilton Jordan was frequently described as the de facto chief of staff due to his involvement in most issues reaching the Oval Office.

[22]By creating a position on the senior White House staff for intergovernmental affairs, Carter was fulfilling a campaign pledge to build closer relations with state and local governments.

[23]Jody Powell had the closest personal relationship to Carter of any member of the senior staff. As Patrick Anderson noted, "Aside from Rosalyn, there is no one Jimmy owes more to on a day-to-day basis than Jody Powell." See "Jody Powell, Press Secretary: A Spokesman in Transition," November 21, 1976, Washington *Post*, p F1.

8. Zbigniew Brzezinski, National Security Advisor[24]
9. James Schlesinger, Energy Advisor[25]

Cabinet Government

As the administration began to take shape, Carter again emphasized open access by the cabinet to reduce the power of the White House staff and to reemphasize the role of the department heads in decision making. Cabinet government, as Carter called it, was an attempt to ensure broad-based participation in decision making and to reduce the concentration of power in the White House that had emerged in the Nixon years. Carter emphasized his commitment to cabinet government stating, "There will never be an instance while I am President, when members of the White House staff dominate or act in a superior position to the members of our Cabinet."[26] By trimming the size and power of the White House staff and building a spokes-of-the-wheel White House organizational structure, Carter endeavored to build a decision system with broad input from multiple sources. The White House staff would no longer control the process, as it had under Richard Nixon.

One of the earliest discussions that Watson had with the outgoing Ford staff involved trimming the White House staff. Carter wanted to reduce the staff to below 500 from its current 542. Ford's staff, however, discouraged further trimming for fear of disrupting key parts of the White House organization. The Ford staff noted that the Ford staff had significantly cut the White House staff from its 640 members in 1974 to the current 542 level. Watson was not convinced and looked for areas to further reduce the staffing level by another 15%.

The Domestic Council Reviewed

In line with Carter's view of a trimmed-down White House staff with fewer policy responsibilities, the role of the Domestic Council was minimized from the earliest stages of the administration. When Watson looked for areas to trim, the Domestic Council was first on the list.

[24]Brzezinski had the dual title of Assistant to the President for National Security and executive director of the National Security Council.
[25]Carter intended to submit to Congress plans for a Department of Energy once his reorganization authority had been granted, with Schlesinger as the nominee for Secretary of Energy. The position of energy advisor was temporary until the Department of Energy was created and was not a permanent White House position.
[26]Joel Havemann, "The Cabinet Band—Trying To Follow Carter's Baton," *National Journal*, July 16, 1977, p 1104.

The first serious mention of a role for the Domestic Council in the Carter White House was broached by Jack Watson in an interview during the transition. He said that there was "a serious question as to whether there is a need to be served by the Domestic Council. Speaking for myself, I have a strong, personal inclination towards a flexible, people-oriented structure. By that I mean those that reflect the personalities, the strengths, and the weaknesses of the people in the structure, rather than the creation of structures which become institutionalized and rigid, irrespective of the strengths and weaknesses of the people around them."[27]

The task of reviewing the White House organizational structure during the transition fell to Harrison Wellford, with the assistance of James Gammill, Richard Hardin, and David Woodham. A number of White House units were immediately targeted for elimination by Wellford's group, including the Foreign Intelligence Advisory Board, the Office of Telecommunications Policy, and the Energy Resources Council. Each of these units could be readily absorbed by existing federal agencies according to the transition team. The Domestic Council, which Watson had recommended for elimination, was less easily absorbed since its mission was to coordinate domestic initiatives among the federal agencies and develop policy guidance. The discussion on the elimination of the Domestic Council soon became submerged within the discussions over restructuring the Domestic Council.

Restructuring the Domestic Council

Several possibilities for restructuring the Domestic Council were considered, in addition to Watson's proposal for simple elimination. One possibility considered was to continue using both the Domestic Council and the Economic Policy Board, which Ford had created, to define administration policy. Under this scenario, the White House would provide staff to the Domestic Council and the Economic Policy Board.[28] Another possibility was to retain only the Domestic Council, perhaps under a new name, whose focus would be narrowly defined within domestic policy. The name *Social Policy Board* was bandied about but eventually discarded. However, another possibility was to restructure the Domestic Council within a broader context to include economic issues, both domestic and foreign, and trade issues.

[27]Dom Bonafede, "Carter Staff Is Getting Itchy to Move to Washington, *National Journal*, October 30, 1976, p 1544.
[28]Dom Bonafede, "The Carter White House—The Shape Is There, But No Specifics," *National Journal*, December 25, 1976, p 1801.

Separating Domestic Policy from Economic Policy

As the transition team was reviewing the possibilities for structuring the domestic and economic policy components of the White House staff, a totally separate group was developing a proposal to move economic policy out of the White House. Michael Blumenthal and Charles Schultze, who had advised Carter during the campaign on economic policy and who were both nominated to Cabinet-level posts, had prepared an evaluation of economic policy making that was separate from the official transition team review. They prepared a recommendation to create the Economic Policy Group (EPG), which would include the Treasury secretary, Council of Economic Advisors chairman, Office of Management and Budget director, and the secretary of State. The national security advisor and the domestic policy advisor would serve as ex officio members, attending all meetings.[29] The Economic Policy Group was merely the Economic Policy Board with a new name.

By early February the discussion on the organizational structure for policy making was renewed. Eizenstat supported splitting the domestic policy function and creating an Economic Policy Group to manage economic policy. However, he was less concerned with the policy implications of a separate economic policy unit than with the political and public relations implications of the specific unit designed by Blumenthal and Schultze. Eizenstat wanted the EPG membership broadened from the Blumenthal/Schultze proposal to include the secretary of Housing and Urban Development, who was black.[30] Hamilton Jordan agreed with Eizenstat on the membership issue and noted in a memo to Carter on February 1, 1977, that "we will get continual criticism from black leaders for not having a black person who participates directly in the formulation of economic policy. As a solution, I would recommend Pat Harris [Secretary of HUD] for inclusion on the Executive Committee on the economic policy group because she is black...."[31]

Carter agreed, noting that it was entirely consistent with his policy of bringing women and minorities into policy-making positions. By adding Patricia Roberts Harris to the Economic Policy Group, Carter had been true to his word and, perhaps more important, broadened his political base within

[29]Memorandum for the President-Elect from Messrs. Blumenthal and Schultze, "Organization of Economic Policy Making," January 6, 1977, Box FG 95, Jimmy Carter Presidential Library, Atlanta, Georgia.
[30]Memorandum for Rick Hutcheson from Stu Eizenstat, "Hamilton Jordan Memo re Economic Policy Group Membership," February 3, 1977, Box 279, Reorganization File, Jimmy Carter Presidential Library, Atlanta, Georgia.
[31]Memorandum to the President from Hamilton Jordan, "Economic Policy Group Membership," February 1, 1977, Box 270, Reorganization File, Jimmy Carter Presidential Library, Atlanta, Georgia.

the African American community.[32] The final membership on the Economic Policy Group (EPG) was broadened to include the secretaries of State, Treasury, Commerce, Labor, HUD, Council of Economic Advisors, Office of Management and Budget, and the National Security Council. Stu Eizenstat would serve as an ex officio member as the original plan had proposed. However, not only was the membership of the Economic Policy Group changed from its Ford days, but its staff was dramatically altered. Rather than operating out of the White House, as it had under Ford, the Blumenthal/Schultze proposal moved the staff to the Treasury Department.[33]

The staffing change from the White House to Treasury by the Economic Policy Group ultimately proved to be beneficial to Eizenstat, for it allowed the domestic policy office to capture the policy leadership role in the White House. With the Economic Policy Group in Treasury, no other unit vied for control over the domestic agenda.

The Domestic Policy Office

Once the Economic Policy Group had moved to the Treasury Department in February, the domestic policy office became the focal point of the domestic agenda. However, the debate during the transition over the degree to which economic policy and domestic policy should be joined had overshadowed many of the essential questions about the domestic policy office. No final decision on the title of or role of the domestic policy staff had been made. Although Stuart Eizenstat had been named director of the domestic policy staff and had been given the title Assistant to the President for Domestic Affairs, the same title that both John Ehrlichman under Nixon and Jim Cannon under Ford had been given, the role of the domestic policy staff had not been defined. The only formal indication of a continuation of a role for the domestic policy unit in the Carter White House emerged in a memo written by Greg Schneiders of the transition team on the organization of White House staff, noting that the role of the Domestic Council would be continued. Schneiders envisioned domestic policy to continue to be managed through the Domestic Council (Figure 4.2), national security policy to continue to be managed through the National Security Council, and economic policy to be managed by the Council of Economic Advisors.[34]

[32]Carter received 94% of the black vote during the 1976 election, including a record turnout by black voters.

[33]Memorandum for the President from Mike Blumenthal and Charlie Schultze, "Proposed Organization of an Economic Policy Group," February 12, 1977, Box 271, Reorganization File, Jimmy Carter Presidential Library, Atlanta, Georgia.

[34]Memorandum to Hamilton Jordan, Jack Watson, Stu Eizenstat, Stephen Hess from Greg Schneiders, "Organization of White House Staff and Executive Office of the President,"

- President
- Vice President
- Attorney General
- Secretary of the Treasury
- Secretary of the Interior
- Secretary of Agriculture
- Secretary of Commerce
- Secretary of Transportation
- Secretary of HEW
- Secretary of HUD
- Secretary of Labor
- Director of OMB
- Chairman of the Council of Economic Advisors
- Administrator of EPA
- Director of Action

Figure 4.2   Domestic Council, 1977–1978

In the absence of a final decision during the transition on the role of the Domestic Council, Eizenstat built on Schneider's recommendation and quickly moved to establish a presence for the Domestic Council and the White House domestic policy office. The Domestic Council was reconstituted with the domestic policy office serving the council's staffing needs. As it had under Nixon and Ford, the Domestic Council included the domestic cabinet, with the president serving as chair. By reestablishing the Domestic Council to oversee the administration's domestic agenda, the Domestic Policy Office was immediately given a role within the policy process.

With the Domestic Council officially active, Eizenstat tried to create a new image for the domestic policy office by giving it a new name, the Domestic Policy Staff (DPS). Under the two previous administrations, it had been referred to simply as the Domestic Council staff. Eizenstat then divided the domestic policy office into functional areas, including internal administration, energy and natural resources, agriculture and rural development, urban affairs, special projects—academics, human resources, economics/business, and federal regulations.

He melded various policy areas together to reduce the number of staff that would be needed, and he added a section on civil rights. As Gary Reichard noted, "Blacks looked toward the Carter administration with genuine

---

(continued)

November 29, 1976, Special Projects Collection, Box 4, Jimmy Carter Presidential Library, Atlanta, Georgia.

hope," and Eizenstat sought to ensure that the White House oversaw the administration's efforts in civil rights.[35] Eizenstat's efforts in building civil rights into the domestic agenda were supported by White House Counsel Robert Lipshutz, who aggressively attempted to add women and minorities to the ranks of federal judges. According to Lipshutz, "we really searched out for qualified women, qualified blacks, qualified Hispanics to make sure that the affirmative action goals of the president were met in practice."[36]

Developing a Policy Agenda for the Domestic Policy Office

The size of the Domestic Policy Staff was ultimately fixed at 18–20 professionals and ten secretarial, a number significantly below either the Nixon or Ford years. Not surprisingly, Eizenstat saw the role of the domestic policy office quite differently than his predecessors had. John Ehrlichman had used the office to frame the domestic agenda for the Nixon administration and to ensure that departmental policies were in line with that agenda. Jim Cannon had used the office for long-range planning for the Ford administration. Stuart Eizenstat took yet another approach to the domestic policy office by using it as a White House think tank and to manage priority, or firefighting, issues for the president. In large part, Eizenstat resisted the long-range planning role of the domestic policy office at the outset of the administration, choosing instead to focus on firefighting. He supported Carter's commitment to cabinet government and chose not to interfere with departmental policy making. As one of Eizenstat's staff noted of the domestic policy office, "We put this staff together in order to function within the parameters of Carter's very strong commitment to the departments."[37]

During the early weeks of the administration, Eizenstat's office was particularly concerned with immediate issues facing the administration, such as developing the executive order to pardon Vietnam War draft evaders, developing a position on U.S. landing rights for the supersonic *Concorde*, curbing the immigration of illegal aliens, and resolving an interagency dispute over welfare reform. Once the administration had moved into full swing, the domestic policy office began to focus on reviewing departmental initiatives. But their role in policy development was tempered by several internal problems within the White House.

The primary problem was that Eizenstat was involved in a myriad of policy discussions with other White House staff, particularly a group known as the triumvirate, that often dominated his time. His absence from the day-to-day

---

[35]Gary W. Reichard, "Early Returns: Assessing Jimmy Carter," *Presidential Studies Quarterly*, Volume 20, Number 3, Summer 1990, p 608.

[36]Exit interview of Robert Lipshutz, September 29, 1979, p 32, Jimmy Carter Presidential Library, Atlanta, Georgia.

[37]Ervin C. Hargrove, *Jimmy Carter as President*, pp 39–40.

activities in the domestic policy office grew more severe when he was pulled into a task force created by Harrison Wellford to oversee the reorganization planning for the Executive Office of the President and the White House staff. But an equally difficult problem for the domestic policy office was Jack Watson's control of the policy development process. The domestic policy office was responsible only for the review of departmental policy proposals and not for the initial development of the proposals by the departments.

The Triumvirate: Reviewing Reorganization

As he promised during the campaign, Carter created a management structure that brought multiple participants into the decision-making process. This was intended to foster "open government" and to reduce isolated decision making in the White House. As a result, Eizenstat became part of a larger White House group called the *triumvirate*, a group that included the Domestic Policy Staff, the Office of Management and Budget under Bert Lance, and the cabinet secretariat under Jack Watson. The triumvirate was charged with ensuring that domestic initiatives included both White House staff and cabinet input and satisfied the budgetary controls for reducing the deficit put in place by the Office of Management and Budget.

The triumvirate was also charged with preparing the reorganization authority request that Carter planned to submit to Congress. This had been a key component of Carter's campaign and one that would be relatively easy to accomplish. It therefore became a priority issue for the new administration and moved to the top of the pile of issues that the triumvirate addressed. The Office of Management and Budget became the managing partner of the triumvirate's reorganization task force, with Harrison Wellford, now associate director of the Office of Management and Budget, assigned to manage the reorganization.

Wellford had directed the reorganization study during the transition and prepared a report entitled, "White House Study Project, Report No. 2." Eizenstat quickly became a central player in Wellford's reorganization planning. In a transition memo written on January 11, 1977, Wellford wrote Eizenstat that a draft of the president's request for reorganization authority was nearly complete and would be sent to him "in the next couple of days" to discuss "some items of mutual interest."[38] Within six days after the inauguration, Wellford had assembled a complete package of the material seeking Congressional extension of the president's reorganization authority and

[38]Memo from Harrison Wellford to Stuart Eizenstat, "Proposed Reorganization Authority," January 11, 1977, Box 270, Reorganization File, Jimmy Carter Presidential Library, Atlanta, Georgia.

sent it to Eizenstat for review.[39] The package, proposing that the president submit to Congress draft legislation to extend the 1939 Reorganization Act, recommended:

1. extension of the authority for four years from date of enactment;
2. authorization for presidential amendment or withdrawal of a plan within 30 calendar days of its transmittal to Congress;
3. deletion of the requirement that not more than one plan be submitted every 30 days; and
4. deletion of the requirement that potential savings that result from the proposal be enumerated in the plan.

The reorganization request was subsequently forwarded to Congress in the package that Wellford had recommended. With little debate, Congress approved the reorganization request on March 31. The bill was strongly supported by Thomas "Tip" O'Neill, Speaker of the House, and easily moved through both the Democratically controlled House and Senate.

The grant of reorganization authority allowed Carter to restructure both the departments and the Executive Office of the President (EOP). The cabinet was to be restructured to include a new Department of Energy and a new Department of Education, as promised during the campaign. The Executive Office of the President was to be trimmed to reflect an increased reliance on the departments for policy development. The transition team, and the subsequent OMB reorganization team, recommended that the policy development structure be refocused from the White House to the departments in order to "eliminate their penchant for empire building and subversion of cabinet initiatives."[40]

The push by Michael Blumenthal and Charles Schultze to move the economic policy function from the White House to Treasury through the Economic Policy Group was directly in line with the reorganization team's recommendations. The Domestic Council appeared to be the next target for elimination or transfer, but Eizenstat moved to maintain its role as the president's primary advisor on domestic affairs.

Options for Reorganizing the Domestic Council

Throughout the spring of 1977 the Wellford task force, formally known as the President's Reorganization Project, studied proposals for the various

[39]Memo from Harrison Wellford to Stuart Eizenstat, "Reorganization Authority," January 26, 1977, Box 270, Reorganization File, Jimmy Carter Presidential Library, Atlanta, Georgia.
[40]Dom Bonafede, "Reorganization Is Easiest When It's Done At Home," *National Journal*, April 23, 1977, p 626.

Eizenstat's broad policy role, from child abuse to airline deregulation, involved primarily a role of management and budget control. Few domestic programs fit any other rubric. With the exception of a few issues such as the pardon of the Vietnam War draft evaders, the activities of the Domestic Policy Staff focused on broad issues of reorganization, management, and budget. The activities of the Domestic Policy Staff were directly in line with Carter's direction for the administration. In a question-and-answer session at the State Department at the end of May, 1977, Carter stated that, "I am deeply committed to the principle that we ought to have an efficient, economical, well-organized, well-managed federal government."[59] The American public seemed to approve of this strategy, giving Carter a 66% approval rating during the first six months of his administration.[60]

Watson's Control of Policy Development

Throughout the first six months of the administration, the domestic policy office focused on departmental management issues, reorganization, and a few policy issues stemming from the campaign, such as the pardon for Vietnam draft evaders. Carter's campaign pledge for cabinet government had essentially removed the Domestic Policy Staff from developing broad policy goals for the administration or initiating policy proposals. That role was reserved for the departments. According to one staffer in the domestic policy office, their job was simply to "review proposals that are sent to him [the president] for his comment."[61] Those reviews, however, centered on fiscal and management constraints rather than the degree of political consistency in departmental initiatives.

But by mid-1977, it became apparent that cabinet government was leading to chaos in the administration. An internal White House memo referred to the "free for all" in domestic policy.[62] Departments were pursuing their own programs with little oversight from the White House. In a "personal and confidential" memo to the president, political advisor Hamilton Jordan strongly advised a review of departmental power. "We continue to have a major problem in the coordination of the goals and objectives of your administration. Each cabinet officer is pursuing programs and goals independent of

---

[59]Memorandum to the President, "Decision Analysis Report" from the President's Reorganization Project," from Sam Carradine et al., May 31, 1977, Jimmy Carter Presidential Library, Atlanta, Georgia.
[60]Gallup Poll in February 1977 and July 1977.
[61]Letter from Daniel Beard to Ronald Schultz, February 8, 1977, Box FG 82, Jimmy Carter Presidential Library, Atlanta, Georgia.
[62]Memo from Al Stern to Bert Carp, "Comments on the EOP Reorganization Project," June 27, 1977, File FG 6-7, Jimmy Carter Presidential Library, Atlanta, Georgia.

one another and oblivious to the political interrelationships of their programs," Jordan said.[63]

In order to curb the free for all, the process for managing domestic policy had to be revised. This occurred during the summer of 1977 when the
White House staffing structure underwent a major overhaul. The primary
staff change involved Jack Watson, who had been charged with domestic policy development. Watson had the job of cabinet secretary, which included
working with the cabinet to identify policy concerns and to initiate policy
proposals. After identifying issues of concern, Watson assembled groups of
cabinet officers, known as *cabinet clusters*, to develop policy proposals.[64]
Carter put Watson in charge of the process to ensure a cabinet-based rather
than White House-based policy development process.

Watson was responsible for appointing cabinet members to the clusters,
although he often found that the process was complicated when cabinet officers tried to appoint themselves. One member of the White House staff joked
that "Every time there was a major issue, everyone flocked to the spotlight
and crowded it."[65] The diverse, and often exceedingly large, cluster groups
frequently disagreed on their own agenda and on the policy initiatives on the
table, leading to lengthy debates and often poorly defined proposals.

The policy proposals developed by the clusters were then given to
Eizenstat's Domestic Policy Staff for review, a review that focused on limited
management criteria. The review included a recommendation for Carter to
approve, disapprove, or seek more information from the department or cabinet cluster that assembled the policy proposal. The cabinet cluster policy
development process had in large part mirrored the spokes-of-the-wheel
staffing structure in the White House. The cabinet clusters were the spokes
of the wheel with Jack Watson at the center of the wheel. Watson gave little
direction to the spokes, allowing each spoke, or cabinet cluster, to operate
autonomously. Watson provided little direction on administration priorities
nor did he reinforce campaign themes. The result was an uncoordinated and
unsupervised policy process. The policy process, though, was absolutely in
line with Carter's theme of cabinet government.

Watson's New Cycle of Activity

In August, 1977, the White House staff underwent a major reorganization.
Headlines flashed across the country's newspapers about a staff shakeup.

[63]Memo, Hamilton Jordan to Jimmy Carter, March 1977, Box 34, Hamilton Jordan Files,
Jimmy Carter Presidential Library, Atlanta, Georgia.
[64]Cabinet clusters were ad hoc groups of cabinet officers devoted to specific policy issues, such
as welfare reform. Cabinet clusters were assembled for issues with multiple or overlapping
jurisdictions. Membership, which generally involved only a few cabinet members, varied
depending on the issue.
[65]Interview with Bill Cable.

Watson's job was essentially taken out of the policy development loop and his job narrowly redefined to manage cabinet meetings, to follow-up on departmental directives from the president, and to manage implementation with state and local governments. The task of managing the cabinet clusters and policy development was moved to Eizenstat, who became the big winner in the shakeup. Watson never publicly complained about the restructuring and matter of factly explained the change, saying that the "administration was moving into a new cycle of activity, where there is more to be monitored, more implemental activity that needs White House attention and the presidential presence."[66]

With Watson no longer controlling the cabinet clusters, Eizenstat consolidated the policy development and review process within the domestic policy office. His first move was to officially gain authority to manage the domestic agenda.[67] That authority was provided through a presidential directive that established the Domestic Policy Review System (DPRS). The DPRS gave the Domestic Policy Group responsibility for "priority setting" and "coordination" in policy issues.[68] Eizenstat, who created the DPRS structure, was given the authority to coordinate the domestic policy process and manage the administration's domestic policy agenda. In essence, the Domestic Policy Review System not only formalized the consolidation of Watson's original responsibilities with that of Eizenstat, but gave added weight to the White House for domestic policy management.

While the White House had consolidated its power and tightened control over the policy process, the departments had lost their independence in policy setting with the August, 1977, shakeup. The cabinet cluster process that Watson had instituted was continued under Eizenstat but with greater oversight by White House staff. Cabinet clusters were subsequently created by Eizenstat's staff and their policy proposals tightly guided by the Domestic Policy Staff. Each cluster was assigned one associate director, one to five assistant directors, and one or more secretaries from the Domestic Policy Staff, to manage the cluster activity.[69] The Domestic Policy Staff set the meeting time and meeting agenda and created the perception if not the reality of control by holding all meetings in the Roosevelt Room of the west wing of the White House. The domestic agenda had moved from cabinet-based to White House-based in barely six months.

[66]Dom Bonafede, "Watson and His Crew Work Out Their Double Role," *National Journal*, September 17, 1977, p 1442.
[67]Interviews with Stuart Eizenstat and his assistant, Joe Onek.
[68]Memo, Stu Eizenstat to Harrison Wellford and A. D. Frazier, "Domestic Policy Review System," September 11, 1977, Box FG 271, Reorganization Folder, Jimmy Carter Presidential Library, Atlanta, Georgia.
[69]Interview with Bert Carp.

The Free for All: Departmental Independence in Policy Making

Once Eizenstat had gained the authority to coordinate the domestic agenda, he continued to reduce the departments' independence in policy making. For example, in September, barely a month after Carter had established the Domestic Policy Review System, the Domestic Policy Staff targeted key members of the cabinet who had openly challenged the White House. The target departments exemplified the free for all that Jordan had complained about.

One cabinet member, Bob Bergland, secretary of Agriculture, had consistently been a thorn in the administration's side as he pursued higher price supports than the White House or OMB wanted. Bergland, a wheat farmer, had chastised Carter for his failure to live up to a campaign promise at the Iowa State Fair made on August 25, 1976, to "make sure that our support prices are at least equal to the cost of production."[70] Bergland was subsequently called to task in a memo in which Carter said "the Secretary of Agriculture must weigh and balance interests represented in other parts of the Executive Branch."[71] In other words, Bergland had failed to consider either the budgetary or political implications of policies that encouraged higher price supports. Carter went on to say in the strongly worded memo that Eizenstat would be working closely with Bergland on any policy issues in the future. "The Secretary of Agriculture," Carter said, "in consultation with the Domestic Policy Staff, will inform me of policies adopted and actions taken..." Bergland had been effectively told to work closely with Eizenstat on all policy issues and to ensure that all policy proposals meet the president's goals for fiscal control.

Bergland had not been the only member of the president's cabinet to move in directions at odds with the White House. Brock Adams, secretary of Transportation, lobbied Congress for a mass transit fund, in spite of Carter's objection. Joseph Califano, secretary of Health, Education and Welfare, supported prohibiting smoking in public places, in spite of the political implications of alienating the tobacco lobby.[72] Attorney General Griffin Bell opposed Carter's position on using Comprehensive Employment and Training Act (CETA) funds in church-related schools.[73] Welfare reform was publicly battled out between the secretaries of Agriculture, Housing and Urban Development, and Health, Education and Welfare. Bergland and Harris refused to allow any of their welfare-related programs to be moved to

[70]"1977 Farm Bill Raises Crop Price Supports," *1977 Congressional Quarterly Almanac*, Volume 33, p 417.

[71]Memorandum for the Heads of Executive Departments and Agencies from the President, September 30, 1977, Box FG 96, Jimmy Carter Presidential Library, Atlanta, Georgia.

[72]Joseph Califano, *Governing America* (New York: Simon & Schuster, 1981), p 188.

[73]Griffin Bell, *Taking Care of the Law* (New York: William Morrow and Co., Inc., 1982), p 46.

Califano. Energy policy became an administration nightmare as Michael Blumenthal, Treasury secretary, battled James Schlesinger, energy advisor, for a role in developing the administration's energy plan.

Reining In the Departments

As the cabinet members continued to operate with little coordination, turf battles, and with minimal concern for the best interests of the administration, Eizenstat aggressively moved to reduce departmental autonomy.[74] Throughout the closing months of 1977, Eizenstat reduced departmental independence in policy making, an independence that Carter had encouraged during the campaign in his pledge for "cabinet administration of our government."

In a case in October, 1977, Eizenstat became so concerned about one department that he went to Carter. Eizenstat's concern focused on Brock Adams, who fervently opposed a reorganization decision by OMB to transfer the Coast Guard to a new Border Management Agency. Eizenstat saw Adams' actions as the first of many by cabinet officers who were resisting both the increasing White House authority in policy making and the general reorganization plans. "Concerns such as those Secretary Adams is voicing," Eizenstat said to Carter, "are likely to be repeated by other cabinet officers..."[75] The Adams incident followed on the heels of another flare up between a cabinet officer and the White House in which Housing and Urban Development Secretary Patricia Harris angrily reputed OMB recommendations for her department in front of the president and other cabinet officers.[76] Eizenstat's recommendation to curb such policy disagreements was to continue on the present course and reduce departmental policy independence. Carter agreed.

Nearly a year after the 1977 staff shakeup, problems in policy oversight continued. Carter again tightened his grip over the departments to bring the departments in line with the White House policy agenda. At a two-day cabinet retreat held at Camp David, Maryland, on April 16–17, 1978, Carter reiterated to the department heads his determination to ensure a cohesive administration agenda. Cabinet members were briefed on the current priorities of the administration and told to bring departmental priorities in line with those established by the White House. Department heads, who were urged to work in greater harmony, were again told that Eizenstat's Domestic Policy Staff would manage the administration's domestic agenda and that all

[74]Interview with Benjamin Heineman.

[75]Memo for the President from Stuart Eizenstat, "Secretary Adams' October 17 Memo," October 21, 1977, Box FG 271, Reorganization Folder, Jimmy Carter Presidential Library, Atlanta, Georgia.

[76]Dennis Farney, "Carter's Cabinet: An Inside View," Washington *Post*, September 7, 1977, p A1.

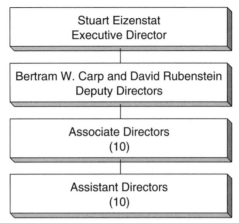

Figure 4.3   Domestic Policy Staff,
                  1978–1979

policy proposals had to be worked through the DPG. As Griffin Bell noted, "In the aftermath, the White House staff assumed more and more power, and the secretaries of most cabinet departments were relegated to a lower level of authority."[77] Cabinet government was being dismantled, and the White House was asserting its role as policy manager. As Eizenstat moved to gain control of the domestic agenda, staff were systematically added to the domestic policy office. By mid-1978, the Domestic Policy Staff had grown to include Eizenstat, a deputy director, an executive assistant director, ten associate directors, ten assistant directors, and assorted other professional and clerical staff (Figure 4.3).

Personnel Management

While Eizenstat was moving on one front to gain control of policy management, Hamilton Jordan and Jack Watson were moving on another front. Jordan and Watson were attacking the problem from the perspective of personnel control of the policy process. Jordan and Watson were convinced that Carter's decision to give the department's autonomy in the hiring of noncivil service staff had been detrimental to the policy process. In their view, too many departmental staff lacked a commitment to Carter's campaign principles of reorganization, efficiency, and fiscal conservatism. On April 24, 1978, cabinet members were sent a memo by Jordan and Watson that said, "The President would like to have in a sealed envelope addressed and delivered to him your own frank evaluation and assessment of the presidential appoint-

---

[77]Griffin Bell, *Taking Care of the Law*, p 46.

ments in your department."[78] The second phase of White House assertion of policy control was underway.

Cabinet Meetings

By May, 1978, cabinet meetings were being refocused from the "show-and-tell" concept in which cabinet officers reviewed their key activities during the past weeks or months, to a "this is what you are going to do" concept. Typical show-and-tell cabinet meetings included such mundane discussions as Secretary of the Interior Cecil Andrus's discussion that "he had just returned from several days in the west and was fully confirmed in his opinion that Washington, D.C., is not the real world" and Secretary of Labor Ray Marshall's discussion of the Geneva Conference for the International Labor Organization.[79]

The new design for cabinet meetings abolished the show-and-tell nature and instituted policy and political direction. Major sections of the cabinet meetings were subsequently devoted to the political consequences of issues and departmental positions. Politics had become a major thrust of cabinet meetings as mid-term elections drew closer and Carter's policies became the subject of increasing Republican attack.[80]

A New Approach to Policy Making

Although the Camp David meetings in April, 1978, had pointedly focused on departmental independence and Carter's decision to give the White House staff greater control over the policy process, the departments continued to operate autonomously. In an internal review of continued departmental independence, White House staff chronicled case after case in which the departments were moving with little or no White House direction or coordination. The review cited a host of problems with the departments, including

1. Department of Energy briefing of Hill staffers, press, and industry before briefing Carter and OMB staff.
2. Assistant Secretary of Energy sent a letter to Congress supporting $20 million beyond the president's budget for additional energy assistance to lesser developed nations.

[78]Memo to Members of the Cabinet from Hamilton Jordan and Jack Watson, "Follow Up On Cabinet Meeting," April 24, 1978, Box FG 41, Cabinet 1978 Folder, Jimmy Carter Presidential Library, Atlanta, Georgia.
[79]Minutes of the Cabinet Meeting, June 20, 1977, Jimmy Carter Presidential Library, Cabinet Folder, Atlanta, Georgia.
[80]Memo to Hamilton Jordan from Anne Wexler, "Meeting with Representatives of the Cabinet," May 4, 1978, Box FG 10, Jimmy Carter Presidential Library, Atlanta, Georgia.

3. Urban Parks Initiative by HUD was sent to Senator Proxmire before legislation had been cleared by OMB.
4. General Canady of the Army testified before the House Armed Services Committee during authorizations hearings that the Army needed the new Tactical Transport Aircraft (AMST) which was terminated in the 1979 budget. This is a $100 million program for FY 1979.
5. Admiral Holloway, Chief of Naval Operations, testified before the House Appropriations Committee that FY 1979 budget should include a nuclear powered aircraft carrier ($2.5 billion) and a nuclear AEGIS cruiser at $1.2 billion. Both were denied by Carter.
6. HEW did not submit to OMB 40 amendments to the House for reauthorization of the Elementary and Secondary Education Act. Several of these amendments contradict the administration's established policy.
7. Califano testified before the Senate Subcommittee on Public Assistance in support of... $1 billion not in the budget.
8. Ersa Poston, Civil Service Commissioner, testified before Senate Finance Committee that she opposed the Treasury Department's approved position not to tax employees who are provided educational benefits from employers.[81]

As the departments continued to ignore White House direction during the spring of 1978, Eizenstat began to urge Carter to further tighten control over the departments. Hamilton Jordan concurred with Eizenstat's recommendation and separately pursued a strategy for personnel management at the sub-cabinet level. Jordan and his deputy, Tim Kraft, required political appointments to be cleared by the White House. Department heads no longer had unbridled discretion in their appointments. Cabinet government, as described by Carter at the outset of his administration, was rapidly deteriorating if not totally abandoned by mid-1978.

During the next year Carter grew increasingly disenchanted with his cabinet, blaming them for his sagging public opinion ratings. The often-disparate policies that cabinet officers continued to support were politically untenable to Carter. His solution was to restructure his cabinet. He had already restructured his White House staff (Figure 4.4) and his White House staff-cabinet operating relationship. The next obvious move was to restructure the cabinet itself.

On July 19 and 20, 1979, Carter fired Joseph Califano (HEW), Michael Blumenthal (Treasury), James Schlesinger (Energy), and Brock Adams (Transportation). Griffin Bell (Justice) resigned and Patricia Roberts Harris (HUD) was moved to replace Califano at HEW (Figure 4.5). As Carter

[81]Memo to Anne Wexler from Bo Cutter, May 5, 1978, Jimmy Carter Presidential Library, Atlanta, Georgia.

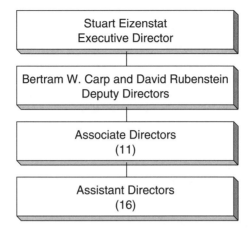

Figure 4.4   Domestic Policy Staff,
1979–1980

admitted, "I had delegated too much authority to my cabinet members."[82] He simultaneously promoted Hamilton Jordan to White House chief of staff.[83] Cabinet government had disappeared, and the White House staff was returning to the hierarchical structure that Carter had originally shunned. The move was welcomed throughout the White House, however. As Hamilton Jordan noted in a memo to Dick Cheney, Ford's chief of staff, who had urged Jordan not to use the spokes-of-the-wheel structure, "Dick—if only I'd listened to you.—A Former Spoke."[84]

Carter's New Cabinet

The redesigned cabinet provided Carter the chance to regain control over the policy process and rebuild public support for the administration, particularly crucial to his reelection efforts. Eizenstat, as were all of the senior White House staff, was removed from direct access to Carter and placed under Jordan.

In essence, this gave Eizenstat greater control over the policy process. Carter, who began to focus on the election, was less interested in policy issues than he was at the start of the administration, and he was eager to delegate to Eizenstat greater control over policy decision making. Carter's focus on

[82]Jimmy Carter, *Keeping Faith* (New York: Bantam Books, 1982), p 117.
[83]Jordan's elevation to chief of staff scored high marks among White House staff, but lower marks in Congress. Many saw Jordan as too young and inexperienced to manage the White House and serve as the president's primary spokesman. See Burton I. Kaufman, *The Presidency of James Earl Carter* (Abilene, Kansas: University of Kansas Press, 1993), p 146.
[84]Dom Bonafede, "Jordan's New Role Signals An End to Cabinet Government," *National Journal*, August 18, 1979, p 1356.

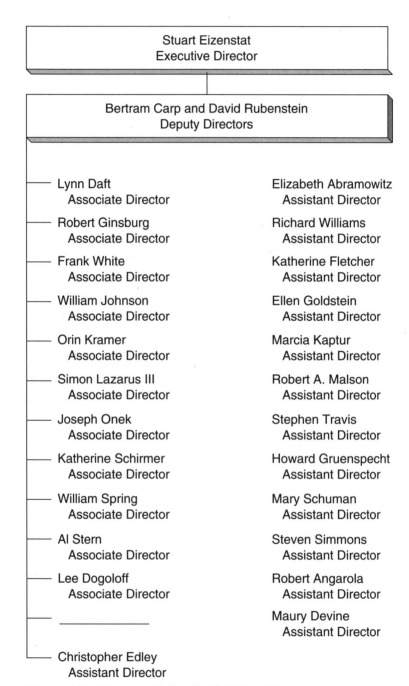

Figure 4.5   Domestic Policy Staff, 1979–1980

domestic policy issues became nearly nonexistent by the last months of the administration, as the Iranian hostage crisis dominated the White House. On November 5, 1979, Iranians stormed the U.S. embassy in Teheran and held its occupants hostage. The administration's response was to impose economic and diplomatic sanctions on Iran but not to pursue military action. Not until April, 1980, did Carter order a military rescue mission for the hostages. The mission failed.

The failed rescue mission left Carter open to ridicule not only from the Republicans, but from Democrats as well. Public support fell dramatically for Carter. According to one poll taken soon after the failed rescue attempt, more people supported the Democratic challenger, Senator Edward Kennedy, than supported the president.[85] Managing domestic policy fell to Stu Eizenstat as Carter became increasingly preoccupied with the hostage crisis and the elections (Figure 4.6). But little moved forward as the White House focused on Iran. Hamilton Jordan later wrote a book on the hostage crisis, simply referring to it as "the crisis."[86] It was a crisis that consumed the president and relegated domestic policy development and oversight to a distant back burner.

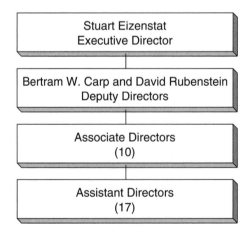

Figure 4.6   Domestic Policy Staff,
1980–1981

[85]Burton L. Kauffman, *The Presidency of James Earl Carter* (Abilene, Kansas: University of Kansas Press, 1993), p 171.
[86]Hamilton Jordan, *Crisis* (New York: G. P. Putnam's Sons, 1982).

Conclusion

The 1980 elections proved disastrous for Jimmy Carter. The public failed to return him to office and instead ushered in the two-term governor of California, Ronald Reagan, to the Oval Office. The failure of Carter to secure the White House for a second term reflected public dissatisfaction with Carter's handling of rampant inflation, increased unemployment, rising oil prices, the Iranian hostage crisis, and deteriorating U.S.-Soviet relations.

Stu Eizenstat had successfully gained control over the domestic agenda by the 1980 elections, but Carter himself had failed to gain control over economic issues and, in particular, the Iranian crisis. Although the domestic agenda had dominated the early part of the administration, by mid-point economic affairs and later foreign affairs overshadowed domestic affairs.

To his credit, Stuart Eizenstat brought the disparate pieces of the domestic puzzle together and formed a coherent policy process. Cabinet government had failed but Eizenstat had been able to revitalize the domestic agenda and rebuild a coordinated policy structure. The Domestic Policy Staff had served the president well and provided the administration clear direction and coordination. Had the domestic policy office been firmly in control of both the economic and domestic agendas from the outset of the term, perhaps the economic problems that beset the administration could have been resolved. The Iranian hostage crisis, however, would most likely have brought down the administration in spite of strong domestic and economic agendas. Perhaps the strongest lesson learned during the Carter years for managing the domestic agenda was that the White House domestic policy office must be firmly in place with clear lines of authority when the administration takes office, and that authority must include broad oversight of departmental initiatives. Writing in 1980 to the next administration, two top Carter departmental appointees urged that the White House must give "the permanent government the necessary direction and leadership."[87] Such leadership must be constant, regardless of crisis issues that may dominate the president's time.

Carter's original decision to dilute the authority of the domestic policy office led to departmental initiatives that lacked symmetry within the agenda and often proved at odds with Carter's political agenda. Ronald Reagan did not make the same mistakes and created a powerful domestic policy office that was far more successful than Carter's at coordinating the domestic agenda.

---

[87]Ben W. Heineman, Jr. and Curtis A. Hessler, *Memorandum for the President: A Strategic Approach to Domestic Affairs in the 1980's* (New York: Random House, 1980), p 130.

THE REAGAN REVOLUTION:
THE CONSERVATIVE AGENDA

The election of Ronald Reagan in 1980 ushered in the conservative revolution in American politics and changed the cast of national politics for over a decade. The "Reagan Revolution" aggressively attacked the mounting role of the federal government and decried the increasing nature of the welfare state. In contrast to Jimmy Carter who wanted to streamline the delivery of services and improve government efficiency, Reagan sought a complete overhaul of the system that reduced federal services and, in many cases, turned those services over to the states.

Reagan's conservative political views had been well known in political circles for nearly twenty years. He had gained national attention in 1964 when he campaigned for conservative presidential candidate Barry Goldwater. Goldwater, who was challenging the incumbent president Lyndon Johnson, was preaching a message of bloated bureaucracy and fiscal irresponsibility. In late October, 1964, Reagan gave a nationally televised speech, paid for by Goldwater's fundraisers, that extolled the virtues of conservatism in national affairs and of the problems of "greater government activity in the affairs of the people . . . Barry Goldwater has faith in us. He has faith that you and I have the ability and the dignity and the right to make our own decisions and determine our own destiny."[1] Although Goldwater lost the election in a landslide for Johnson, Reagan had built a sizeable following for his own political future.

Not unexpectedly, two years later Reagan launched his successful campaign for governor of California, a campaign focused on the same conservative themes that he had defined during the Goldwater campaign. During his two terms as governor, Reagan built a reputation for cutting taxes, cutting the size of government, and returning programs to local governments. "During the eight years I think we made the state government less costly, smaller, and more businesslike," he said. "We began to return some of the power and

[1] Ronald Reagan, *An American Life* (New York: Pocket Books, 1990), p 142–43.

taxing authority usurped by the state from local communities back to where they belonged, at the local level."[2]

A Foray into National Politics

His taste for national politics, however, had been whetted by the 1964 campaign. When a number of prominent California Republicans approached him to run as a favorite son candidate in the 1968 California primary, he agreed and carried a significant number of delegates to the national convention. Nixon, who saw Reagan as a potential rival, never included Reagan in postconvention strategy sessions or considered him for a cabinet post. After two terms in the governor's office, Reagan left Sacramento committed to continuing the conservative agenda and began a nationally syndicated radio show and a newspaper column that allowed him to continue to voice his conservative agenda in the national political arena. As the 1976 presidential election drew closer, Reagan decided to challenge Gerald Ford for the Republican party's nomination. He attacked Ford as being too closely tied to Nixon and ran as an "outsider" candidate—a strategy that Carter was similarly pursuing in the Democratic primaries and that he later pursued in the general election against Ford.

While Ford was emphasizing his integrity and leadership during the 1976 primaries, Reagan was repeating his theme of rolling back government, reducing taxes, balancing the budget, and giving power back to the states. When the rollcall vote came at the Republican National Convention in Kansas City, Reagan came within 70 votes of controlling the nomination. The final count gave Reagan 1070 delegates to Ford's 1187 delegates, with 1140 needed to win.

His near-win in Kansas City only encouraged Reagan to believe that his conservative agenda had a place in the national political arena. Within weeks after losing the election, he established an informal campaign organization with Senator Paul Laxalt (R-Nevada) at the helm.[3] For the next three years Reagan moved throughout the nation, courting conservative Republican activists and building bases of party support through extensive speaking engagements. The informal campaign organization later emerged as a formal campaign organization and, in late 1979, Reagan announced his bid for the 1980 Republican presidential nomination. Paul Laxalt moved into the formal role of campaign chairman, and John Sears, who had managed Reagan's 1976 campaign against Gerald Ford, was hired to run the day-to-day operations.

[2]Ibid, p 191.
[3]Laxalt and Reagan had become friends in the 1960s as governors of two adjoining states. Laxalt was elected to the Senate in 1974.

The Reagan Revolution had not only swept in the conservative president, but swept in a new tide in Congress. For the first time since 1954, the Republicans gained control in the Senate and dramatically reduced the Democratic majority in the House. The task of governing for the president-elect had been significantly eased with the change in membership of the 97th Congress.

The Transition

For Ronald Reagan, the task of governing began soon after his electoral landslide as he began to construct the administration that would carry out his mandate. The transition staff that emerged was a combination of campaign staff and campaign advisors (Figure 5.2). Meeting the day after the election at Reagan's Pacific Palisades home, Edwin Meese was moved from campaign chief of staff to transition director; E. Pendleton James became personnel director; congressional relations was headed by William E. Timmons; Richard Allen managed foreign affairs; former Nixon OMB director Caspar Weinberger was brought in to head budget reviews; and Martin Anderson continued as the domestic policy advisor.[13]

The transition team was divided into three broad areas: personnel selection, departmental management reviews, and policy issue reviews. The personnel operation was directed by James while the departmental management reviews came under William Timmons, who had served on both the Nixon and Ford White House congressional liaison staffs. Martin Anderson managed domestic issues policy development, and Richard Allen handled foreign policy.

Personnel Management: Cabinet and White House Staff

The personnel operation took center stage at the outset of the transition process, because ensuring ideological consistency within the senior levels of

- ◆ Edwin Meese III—Director
- ◆ E. Pendleton James—Personnel
- ◆ William E. Timmons—Congressional Relations
- ◆ Richard Allen—Foreign Policy
- ◆ Martin Anderson—Domestic Policy
- ◆ Caspar Weinberger—Budget
- ◆ James Brady—Press Secretary

Figure 5.2   The Reagan Transition Staff

[13]An excellent discussion on the transition is provided in Edwin Meese III, *With Reagan, The Inside Story*, (Washington, D.C.: Regnery Gateway, 1992), p 56.

government was considered the most secure mechanism for achieving programmatic objectives. At the heart of these objectives was reducing the size of government and cutting federal domestic spending. The budget would drive the administration. As Reagan noted of his appointments during the campaign, "Crucial to my strategy of spending control will be the appointment to top government positions of men and women who share my economic philosophy."[14]

But Reagan also wanted to bring people into his administration who would aggressively attack the burgeoning federal regulatory system. Reagan had promised business and industry "regulatory relief" during the campaign, asserting that federal regulation permeated every facet of communications, transportation, the workplace, manufacturing, air, water, and noise standards. He promised to eliminate or repeal many of these regulations and therefore reduce the cost of doing business. Controlling regulatory overload, like controlling the budget, required an army of appointments committed to the Reagan Revolution.

The transition was quickly dominated by the personnel selection process, including cabinet, sub-cabinet, and senior policy makers. Martin Anderson described the personnel selection process as the "most thorough and comprehensive effort undertaken in the history of American transitions" to ensure that appointees did "not betray the policies the campaign was fought on."[15] Personnel selection was managed by Edwin Meese, who divided the process into cabinet and sub-cabinet appointments. Meese worked closely with a small group of Reagan's friends, informally known as the Transition Advisory Group, and with E. Pendleton James, a professional executive search consultant and Reagan loyalist, on the Cabinet selections.[16] James also worked with Meese on the sub-cabinet appointments and eventually moved into the White House as Personnel Director, responsible for all presidential appointments.

The cabinet appointments process began early in the campaign, as it had during the Carter campaign's Talent Inventory Program. In April, 1980, Meese asked James to draw up a plan "for filling the top positions in the government in preparation for a Reagan victory."[17] After the Republican nomination,

[14]Robert J. Samuelson, "Reagan Sticks with His Tax Cut and Spending Policies," *National Journal*, September 20, 1980, p 1574.
[15]Martin Anderson, *Revolution: The Reagan Legacy*, revised edition (Stanford, California: Hoover Institution Press, 1990), p 196.
[16]The transition was provided funding by Congress through the Presidential Transition Act of 1963. The 1976 amendment authorized $2 million for the incoming administration as well as $1 million for the outgoing administration. Reagan raised an additional $1 million in private funds for the transition. James's fee for personnel consulting was paid through private funds.
[17]G. Calvin Mackenzie, "The Reaganites Come to Town: Personnel Selection for a Conservative Administration," paper presented at the American Political Science Association meeting, New York City, September 2, 1981 (revised January 1982), p 3.

James set up the "Reagan–Bush Planning Task Force" in Alexandria, Virginia, and enlarged the staffing operation. The small staff developed priorities for which jobs should be filled first after the election and prepared lists of qualified candidates for each job with detailed resumes of each.[18] The lists included names for both cabinet and sub-cabinet positions.

Reagan had devoted few of his energies during the campaign to the personnel selection process and willingly met with his advisors to sort out names for his cabinet. James provided lists of three names for each cabinet position, in order of preference. At the same time, the California "kitchen cabinet," who referred to themselves as the Transition Advisory Committee, offered their own recommendations for cabinet positions.[19] Many of the recommendations of the two lists overlapped, allowing Reagan to appease his friends without jeopardizing the ideological goals of the transition team.[20] But conflicts between the two groups were minimal, since both approached the cabinet selection process with essentially the same criteria: "One, was he a Reagan man? Two, a Republican? Three, a conservative?"[21]

The final selections involved four members of the Transition Advisory Team moving into the cabinet or senior-level positions: William French Smith to attorney general; Caspar Weinberger to secretary of Defense; Charles Wick to director of the U.S. Information Agency (USIA); and William Casey to the Central Intelligence Agency (CIA). Other senior cabinet appointments included Republican National Committee pointman Drew Lewis to Transportation; former Republican senator Richard Schweiker (a Reagan supporter since 1976) at Health and Human Services; fundraisers Raymond Donovan to Labor; and Donald Regan to Treasury. James allowed some maneuvering in selecting cabinet appointments by allowing Laxalt to bring in James Watt at Interior and James Edwards at Energy; Robert Dole to bring in John Block at Agriculture; and George Bush to bring in Malcolm Baldrige at Commerce. Alexander Haig was brought into State at the strong suggestion of Richard Nixon, who argued in a memo to Reagan that the next secretary of State "must share your general views with regard to the Soviet threat and foreign policy generally. These requirements pretty much limit those who would be considered. Haig meets them all."[22]

Diversity was not ignored in the cabinet but was hardly the subject of serious debate as it had been in the Carter administration. At the suggestion

---

[18]Anderson, *Revolution*, p 198.

[19]The Transition Advisory Committee was chaired by William French Smith, Reagan's personal attorney, and included Justin Dart, Holmes Tuttle, William A. Jorgensen, Theodore E. Cummings, Charles Wick, Alfred Bloomingdale, Jack Wrather, Henry Salvatori, Joseph Coors, Caspar Weinberger, William Wilson, and Daniel Terra. William Casey was an informal member of the group.

[20]Interview with E. Pendleton James.

[21]Cannon, *Reagan*, p 317. Interview with E. Pendleton James.

[22]Lou Cannon, *Reagan, The Role of a Lifetime* (New York: Simon and Schuster, 1991), p 78.

of kitchen cabinet member Alfred Bloomingdale, Reagan brought in a black attorney, Samuel Pierce, at Housing and Urban Development. No women were included in the original cabinet, although Ann McLaughlin, Margaret Heckler, and Elizabeth Dole were added through attrition from the early ranks.

The struggle for power within the White House was mitigated with Reagan's decision to split the responsibilities of managing the White House among his three senior advisors: Edwin Meese, Michael Deaver, and James Baker. Baker, who had managed George Bush's primary campaign, had become a key strategist for the Reagan/Bush campaign and had gained broad support within the Reagan camp.

The troika (named after a Russian vehicle drawn by three horses abreast) that was established divided responsibilities into three clear spheres of influence.[23] Baker, as chief of staff, would manage political affairs, building political coalitions for the Reagan initiatives within Congress and among interest groups. In addition, a wide range of staff would report to Baker, including the personnel office, legal office, speech writers, congressional liaison, press office, and the public liaison. Baker was seen not as a policy maker but as a strategist, responsible for coordinating congressional and public support for the administration.

Meese, as counsellor to the president, was given responsibility for creating the administration's domestic and foreign-policy initiatives. He supervised both the domestic and foreign-policy staffs within the White House and oversaw the Cabinet Secretariat, which provided the link to the departments in policy development and management. Both the domestic policy advisor and the national security advisor were under Meese in the troika's organizational structure.

Deaver, deputy chief of staff, had the day-to-day responsibility for the president's schedule, appointments, travel, the first lady's staff, and the administration of the White House. While their titles varied, each had access to Reagan and were often referred to as the "three deputy presidents."

Departmental Management

The second phase of the transition involved briefing the cabinet nominees on the departments they would soon be running. Timmons assembled briefing teams to prepare reports on each department, including the total number of people within each agency, departmental budget, programmatic mandates of each department, members of Congress with responsibilities for departmental programs, and a list of major issues that would confront the secretary after

---

[23]For an excellent overview of how Reagan's inner circle operated, see George Church, "The President's Men," *Time*, December 14, 1981, p 16ff.

One of Anderson's senior staff, John McClaughry, added another reason for the success of the cabinet councils in maintaining the focus of the domestic agenda. McClaughry described the cabinet councils as "a series of arbitration and mediation panels" that provided the departments access to the White House to plead their cases when policies became territorial turf battles.[33] Anderson's staff in the Office of Policy Development generally resolved interjurisdictional skirmishes before interjurisdictional wars destroyed the focus of the domestic agenda.

Anderson never sought to manage policy development from the White House. The Office of Policy Development was staffed with generalists rather than policy experts, many of whom had moved into the office from the campaign. Anderson's primary goal was to provide direction to the cabinet officers on Reagan's themes throughout the campaign, as framed within the "notebooks," and to allow departments to create their own policy proposals, as long as they were in line with the central themes of the administration and met OMB's stringent budget constraints.

Management of the domestic agenda was supported by the Office of Cabinet Administration, the successor to Carter's Cabinet Secretariat managed by Jack Watson. The Office of Cabinet Administration was run by Craig Fuller, a public relations executive and Deaver, protégé from California. Fuller's job was to schedule full cabinet meetings, set the agenda, and pursue items that Reagan identified for follow-up. Their role was not to become policy managers, as was Watson's original Cabinet Secretariat, but rather to manage the routine operations of cabinet meetings. The Office of Cabinet Administration also handled cabinet requests for meetings made by a department with constituency groups.[34] Fuller maintained an extremely low profile in the White House throughout his tenure and never challenged Anderson's dominance in White House-cabinet affairs. When he moved to the Old Executive Office Building as Bush's vice presidential chief of staff later in the term, Fuller used his experience in cabinet affairs to reach the cabinet on issues for which Bush sought influence.

The Legislative Strategy Group

While Meese and Anderson were managing the policy side of the domestic agenda, Jim Baker and his staff were managing the implementation side.

[33]John McClaughry, "White House Policy-Making Maze; Has the Cabinet Council System Homogenized the Reagan Revolution?," *Washington Times*, February 19, 1985, p A5.
[34]An example was Fuller's decision not to have Reagan meet with members of the National Commission on Excellence in Education. Letter from T. H. Bell to Craig Fuller, "President's Meeting with the National Commission on Excellence in Education," August 12, 1982, Box 4, ED 115900, Ronald Reagan Presidential Library, Simi Valley, California.

Baker's Legislative Strategy Group was responsible for lobbying for public and congressional support for the president's domestic and economic programs. Once the cabinet councils and the Office of Policy Development had completed the policy design, it was handed off to the Legislative Strategy Group to build political support.

Working within the Legislative Strategy Group were Baker, Stockman, Treasury Secretary Donald Regan, Congressional Liaison Max Friedersdorf, and other senior White House staff that might have cause to attend. Meese attended the meetings to brief the group, although he was generally not part of the legislative or political strategy sessions.

The Legislative Strategy Group had the authority to refine or even redesign policy initiatives in order to satisfy the requisite Congressional committees or constituent groups. Their task was to move the proposal forward in the most expeditious means available. Proposals that had been altered were not returned to the cabinet councils for discussion, although the Office of Policy Development was often called upon to handle changes recommended by the Legislative Strategy Group. Baker's goal was to move proposals through the political process as quickly as possible to build Reagan's legislative success record. His theme was flexibility, and policy initiatives were remolded by the Legislative Strategy Group as required.

Changes in the Office of Policy Development

Throughout the first year of the Reagan administration, Anderson's domestic policy operation successfully prevented the departments from seeking broad new legislative programs. This allowed Stockman to focus on reducing budgets within existing programs without fighting the departments on new initiatives. The primary success of the Office of Policy Development was its ability to constantly reinforce the themes of the Reagan administration and the goals articulated by Reagan during the campaign to the cabinet officers. As Anderson and his staff reiterated to the department heads, the primary goal in the domestic agenda was cutting the budget, deregulation, and reducing the size of the federal government.

The cabinet councils also proved to be an extremely effective means of reinforcing the Reagan agenda. By using the Office of Policy Development to staff the councils and to focus the agenda, cabinet councils were limited in their discussions. Anderson's use of the cabinet councils differed significantly from Nixon's original concept, in which the Domestic Council, the forerunner of the cabinet councils, was used for policy initiation and debate. Anderson structured the cabinet councils to focus on reducing overlapping programs, cutting costs within programs, and ending programs that failed to meet the goals of the domestic agenda. While the cabinet councils were often praised as the structure by which Reagan had implemented cabinet government, they were, in fact, a tool to reduce the cabinet's policy independence and a means for the White House to guide departmental objectives.

Those objectives, however, throughout the first year of the administration, were focused on the economic agenda that David Stockman was creating. Anderson was a key member of the economic policy-making group, along with Treasury Secretary Donald Regan, chairman of the Council of Economic Advisers Murray Widenbaum, and David Stockman. The four met every Tuesday morning at 7:30 A.M. in the dining room of the Treasury Department for breakfast. Their task was to reduce programmatic discretionary spending and to reorder spending priorities within the constraints of limited government. Rather than using the White House staff to focus priorities, Anderson became a messenger for Stockman's economic policy and essentially abdicated a policy-making role for the Office of Policy Development. Domestic policy was so closely tied to economic policy that it was difficult to separate the two.

Changes in the Office of Policy Development

After a year at the White House, Anderson decided to return to the academic environment of the Hoover Institution at Stanford University. In the spring of 1982, OMB Deputy Director Edwin Harper, who held the dual titles of Assistant to the President and OMB Deputy Director, was named Assistant to the President for Policy Development, in charge of the cabinet councils and the Office of Policy Development (Figure 5.5). Harper, as had Anderson, had worked in the Nixon administration on John Ehrlichman's staff. Harper and Anderson had shared an office in the Nixon White House, and Anderson had later recruited Harper to work on the Reagan campaign.

Harper made several structural and staff changes to the White House domestic policy operation, naming Roger Porter director of the Office of Policy Development and moving Edwin Gray to director of the newly created Office of Policy Information.[35] Gray, a press secretary in the Reagan administration in Sacramento, ran an in-house press operation for Harper under the new structure. The operating structure of the OPD remained essentially the same, with each of the four assistant directors of the OPD continuing in their roles as the executive secretaries of the cabinet councils. Porter, in spite of his promotion to director of the OPD from assistant director, continued as executive secretary to the economic cabinet council.

[35]Dick Kirschten, "Decision Making in the White House—How Well Does It Serve the President?," *National Journal*, April 3, 1982, p 585.

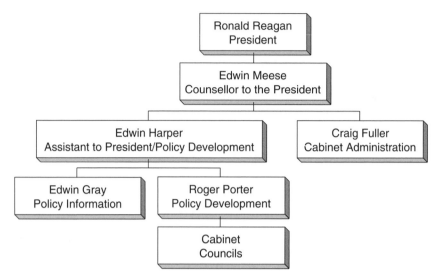

Figure 5.5   Domestic Policy Structure, 1982–1983

While Anderson had used the Office of Policy Development primarily to keep the departments from pursuing new programs and nurturing the senior department staff as Stockman was slashing programs and alienating nearly everyone he came into contact with, Harper intended a more aggressive role for the OPD. Stockman, known for his arrogance, was quick to point out to those in meetings with him that they did not know their own budgets and were completely incapable of understanding OMB's budget projections. Writing in his memoirs, Stockman described a meeting with Caspar Weinberger on the defense budget, noting that, "No one [in the meeting]... knew anything about the defense budget at all. Come to think of it, Weinberger did not know that much either; in his present capacity he was a salesman."[36] Perhaps an even more telling description of Stockman's dominance of economic policy was described in another section of his book:

> We had brow-beaten the cabinet, one by one, into accepting the cuts. It was divide and conquer, not roundtabling. In my haste to expedite the revolution, I had inadvertently convinced the chief executive that budget cutting was an antiseptic process, a matter of compiling innocuous-sounding "half-pagers" and putting them in a neatly tabbed black book... We forced health research cuts on Dick Schweiker at HHS. We stiffed Jack Block with soil conservation cuts at USDA. We shackled Ted Bell with a sweeping retrenchment at the Education Department.[37]

---

[36]David Stockman, *Triumph of Politics* (New York: Avon Books, 1987), p 306.
[37]Ibid, p 123.

Under Harper, the OPD began to move out of the shadow of the Office of Management and Budget and to develop a domestic agenda upon which the economic agenda could be built. OPD began conducting more-detailed policy reviews, working directly with departments rather than primarily with the cabinet councils. And, as he had outside the White House, Harper began a more aggressive approach within the White House. Rather than allowing Meese to represent the domestic policy operation within the senior staff operations, Harper began attending senior staff meetings, Legislative Strategy Group sessions, and the regular Monday update luncheons, used to brief Reagan on issues that might arise in press conferences or public appearances. While Meese remained the official spokesman for domestic policy in the White House, Harper became far more influential in using the OPD as a policy tool than Anderson had been[38] (Figure 5.6).

The rise of Harper through 1982 and 1983 coincided with the fall of Stockman. Both OMB and Stockman came under attack for dramatically underestimating the deficit, in spite of massive programmatic cuts. Stockman's star fell throughout the administration not only because of problems in his own budget estimates, but also because of a published discussion in *The Atlantic Monthly*, November, 1981, in which he said budget deficits could be reduced only with tax increases and cuts in the defense budget. This ran

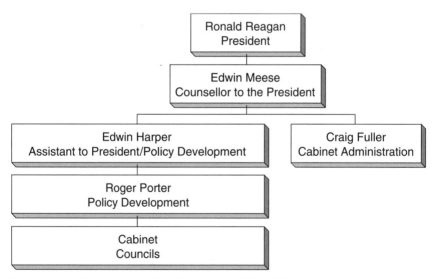

Figure 5.6   Domestic Policy Structure, 1983–1984

[38]For a detailed overview of Harper's management of the cabinet councils, see "Cabinet Councils of Government: Effectively Running the Federal Machine," *Government Executive*, January 1983, pp 20–29.

counter to Reagan's campaign themes and to statements that Stockman had consistently made throughout his term.

As Stockman was losing credibility within the administration and the OMB was losing influence as the driving force in policy decisions, Harper's Office of Policy Development moved in to regain control of the domestic agenda. Throughout 1981, OMB's notorious "black book," which was a looseleaf binder containing reviews and proposed cuts for nearly every departmental program, drove the domestic agenda. OMB, without consultation with the domestic policy office, determined which programs would be slashed and by how much. Harper sought to change the relationship between the economic and domestic policy operations, by using the Office of Policy Development to focus priorities for the administration, establish long-range planning activities, and guide OMB. In 1984 Harper left to return to private life and was replaced by John Svahn, undersecretary of Health and Human Services and a former member of Reagan's California administration.

Svahn was never able to continue Harper's aggressive actions to rebuild the Office of Policy Development as the focus of domestic policy decision making, because Meese preferred decision making to take place in the cabinet councils. As a White House outsider, Svahn was unable to mount the aggressive actions that Harper, as a White House insider, had. An example of Svahn's lack of influence in managing domestic policy was Reagan's decision to sign a farm subsidy bill that OPD opposed after the Agriculture Depart-

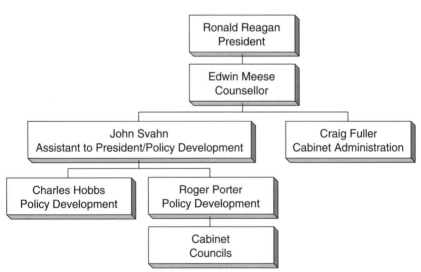

Figure 5.7 Domestic Policy Structure, 1984–1985

ment mounted a substantial lobbying effort in its favor.[39] One observer noted OPD's lack of policy authority that "of late, there have been few complaints of White House bullying on domestic issues."[40] After Meese's departure to the Justice Department, little improved as Svahn was soon undermined by Donald Regan, the new White House chief of staff. The brief hegemony of the White House Office of Policy Development had ended with Harper's departure.

Reagan's Second Term

After four years of moving the conservative agenda forward, Reagan went back to the electorate seeking a second term in office. His opposition was Walter Mondale, Jimmy Carter's vice president, and a little-known member of the House of Representatives, Geraldine Ferraro (D-New York), as Mondale's running mate. In a stunning landslide, Reagan captured every state except for Minnesota (Mondale's home state) and the District of Columbia. The final tally was 54,281,858 votes (525 electoral votes) for Reagan to 37,457,215 votes (13 electoral votes) for Mondale.

When Reagan returned to the White House following his second inauguration, several major changes had taken place in the cabinet and the White House staff. Most significant to the operating structure of the White House was the exit of the Baker/Deaver/Meese troika and the emergence of Donald Regan as chief of staff. Baker exchanged jobs with Regan and moved to head the Treasury Department. Meese took over the Justice Department from William French Smith, who wanted to return to California, and Deaver established a public relations firm in Washington, D.C. The scenario was sparked by Regan, who jokingly said early in the administration, "The only job better than the one I've got now is Baker's."[41] He later mentioned it to Baker and suggested they switch jobs. The issue was dropped but raised again by Regan following Reagan's reelection. Baker agreed at Christmas, and both discussed the issue with Reagan, who approved. Meese and Deaver then decided to pursue their own job changes, rather than work with Regan in the White House.

The divided power structure that had guided the White House for four years was quickly consolidated by Regan, who was named chief of staff. All White House staff reported to Regan, with no one having direct access to Reagan. The structure returned the White House to the Haldeman days, when H. R. Haldeman controlled the Nixon White House with an iron

[39]Dick Kirschten, "Don't Look for Sparks to Fly from White House Domestic Policy Office," *National Journal*, December 10, 1983, p 2566.

[40]Ibid, p 2566.

[41]Ed Magnuson, "Shake-Up at the White House," *Time*, January 21, 1985, p 13.

hand. As columnist Eleanor Clift noted of Regan's job change, "Regan has an advantage Baker never had—that of being No. 1 and Only"[42] (Figure 5.8).

Within weeks after he had taken over, Regan began to replace staff and to restructure the domestic policy apparatus. Although Svahn was retained as domestic policy advisor with responsibility for the Office of Policy Development, Regan dramatically changed the policy process. He changed the name of the Office of Cabinet Affairs to the Cabinet Secretary and replaced Craig Fuller with Alfred Kingon. Kingon, who had served as Regan's assistant secretary for policy planning at the Treasury Department, had strong ties to Regan through two decades that both were on Wall Street. The Cabinet Affairs Office under Kingon was given control over the cabinet councils as a means of ensuring that policy development was firmly within Regan's control.[43]

Roger Porter continued as director of the Office of Policy Development, but an additional office was created with the domestic policy organizational structure. Charles Hobbs, who had acquired expertise in welfare issues at the Department of Health and Human Services, was brought in by Regan to manage the welfare reform proposals. Hobbs was given the title Assistant to the President for Policy Development, with the clear intention that he would oversee the broad spectrum of domestic policy. Porter, who continued to have the responsibility for the Office of Policy Development and to serve as executive secretary to the Cabinet Council on Economic Policy, had shown little interest in welfare or other social policy issues. Hobbs was added to the White House staff to refocus the Reagan Revolution around those social

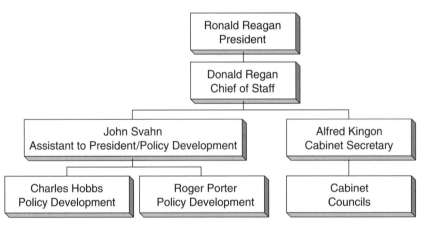

Figure 5.8   Domestic Policy Structure, 1985–1986

[42]Eleanor Clift and Thomas DeFrank, "Regan's White House," *Newsweek*, April 8, 1985, p 23.
[43]The White House, Office of the Press Secretary, "Fact Sheet: Economic Policy Council; Domestic Policy Council," April 11, 1985.

issues that had largely been bypassed during the first term as the economic agenda dominated domestic policy.

Regan subsequently abolished all of the seven original cabinet councils in April 1985 and recreated two new cabinet councils: the domestic policy council and the economic policy council (Figures 5.9 and 5.10).[44] The redesigned structure was designed, according to the White House press release, to afford "better policy coordination, formulation, and implementation."[45] In spite of the press release overview on the functions of the councils, Regan sought the reorganization to gain control of the policy apparatus within the White House. All vestiges of the Baker/Deaver/Meese operation were removed as Regan moved his staff and his structure into place.

The redesigned cabinet council structure reinforced Regan's control over the domestic policy process and also reduced the access points for the cabinet into the White House and to the president. While most cabinet members had participated in four or five cabinet councils under the Meese structure, no member of the cabinet served on both the newly created Domestic Policy and the Economic Policy Council. Regan's explanation for the change in the cabinet council structure centered on Reagan's inability to deal with too many participants in the decision-making process. According to Regan, "the closer focus that the simpler apparatus provided made it easier for him [Reagan] to keep track of the ideas put forward by his Cabinet officers."[46] In reality, the simpler apparatus made it easier for Regan to keep track of the domestic policy proposals put forward by the cabinet officers.

◆ Attorney General—Chair	◆ Treasury—Chair
◆ Interior	◆ State
◆ HHS	◆ Agriculture
◆ HUD	◆ Commerce
◆ Transportation	◆ Labor
◆ Energy	◆ OMB
◆ Education	◆ Trade Representative
◆ OMB	◆ Council of Economic Advisors

Figure 5.9　Domestic Policy Council, 1985　　　**Figure 5.10**　Economic Policy Council, 1985

[44]Gerald M. Boyd, "Reagan Revamping Cabinet Councils; 2 Key Aides Named," *New York Times*, April 12, 1985, p A1.

[45]The White House, "Fact Sheet: Economic Policy Council; Domestic Policy Council," April 11, 1985.

[46]Donald Regan, *For the Record: From Wall Street to Washington* (New York: Harcourt Brace Jovanovich, 1988), p 334.

Domestic Policy Making in the Regan Cabinet Council System

With the fall of David Stockman and his ultimate departure in mid-1985, Regan was able to solidify his control over the policy making process.[47] Although Ed Harper had tried to gain control over domestic policy making, OMB remained a major factor in focusing the agenda. Harper had increased the role of the Office of Policy Development in the policy process, but was unable to overcome the influence of OMB.

By the time Regan moved into the White House, OMB's power had been eroded and James Miller, who succeeded Stockman, had never regained the leverage in policy control that Stockman had. Regan was able to easily restructure the White House policy operation and the White House-cabinet relationship to control the domestic agenda.

The redesigned structure for policy development focused on the Cabinet Affairs Office, rather than the Office of Policy Development. Policy proposals that emerged within the departments were put on the agendas of the appropriate cabinet council, which discussed the proposal and sent back recommendations to the president through the Cabinet Affairs Office.[48] Regan reviewed the recommendations and either sent them back for further revision or moved them into the Oval Office with his own recommendation for Reagan's review.

The Cabinet Affairs Office became the center of White House-cabinet discussions on domestic policy, but tensions mounted within months of the new operation as Kingon was seen as "arrogant" and even "contemptuous" of department staff.[49] Within a year, Kingon had been replaced by Nancy Risque. The structure that Regan had created to narrow the decisions addressed by the cabinet and to reduce access points to Reagan had been eroded by Kingon's relationship with the departments. Cabinet officers began to talk directly with Reagan in cabinet meetings, to call him, and to work to some degree through the Office of Policy Development.

By mid-1985 as Regan was trying to consolidate domestic policy making in the Cabinet Affairs Office, the Office of Policy Development was being further removed from agenda setting as it was relegated to primarily planning and firefighting activities.[50] John Svahn, who continued as the domestic policy advisor, was essentially isolated by Regan from the departments.

---

[47]Stockman left the administration in August, 1985, to join a Wall Street firm. He also signed a $2.4 million contract with Harper and Row to publish a book on his tenure in the Office of Management and Budget. The book, *Triumph of Politics*, was published and then serialized by *Newsweek*.

[48]Interview with Ralph Bledsoe.

[49]Donald Rheem, "White House Says Policymaking Structure Works Well," *Christian Science Monitor*, August 13, 1987, p 1.

[50]David Hoffman, "White House Overhauls Policy Apparatus," *Washington Post*, April 12, 1985, p A12.

Roger Porter, the director of the Office of Policy Development, focused most of his activities on his role as executive secretary of the economic policy cabinet council. Rather than operating as the administration's senior policy manager, Porter increasingly became a bureaucrat within the cabinet council structure. Svahn became so outraged with Porter's abdication from the OPD in favor of his work on the economic policy cabinet council that he reportedly said to Porter, "Who do you work for now?"[51] After a series of battles with Svahn, Porter left the White House at the end of 1985 for a position at Harvard University's Kennedy School of Government. By 1986, the Office of Policy Development had become a nonplayer in the policy process.

Departments were increasingly operating as solo players in the policy making process as the White House was losing control over domestic policy making. A prominent example of departmental independence was the case of the Department of Health and Human Services under Dr. Otis Bowen, appointed by Reagan in November, 1985. Bowen, who had spent thirty years in general medical practice, was committed to including catastrophic health care within the Medicare system. The proposal was strongly opposed by OMB as too costly and heavily lobbied against by the insurance industry with a sizeable interest in medigap insurance.[52] The White House was unable to stop Bowen from continuing in his pursuit of catastrophic health care as he systematically built both constituent and legislative support for expansion of the Medicare system. Reagan was eventually forced by public pressure to support Bowen's proposal, a proposal that had been originally opposed by both the Domestic Policy Council and the Office of Policy Development (Figure 5.11).

As 1986 drew to a close, Regan began to develop a plan to restructure the domestic policy apparatus. Largely under pressure from the New Right, which considered Regan an ally, Regan reactivated the domestic policy office to address the social issues that neither Svahn nor Hobbs had aggressively dealt with. Svahn resigned at the end of 1986. Hobbs continued to manage welfare reform, and, in Svahn's place, Gary Bauer was added. Bauer was brought in as the president's senior domestic policy advisor, Assistant to the President for Policy Development, and was charged with reasserting the revolution's conservative themes.[53] Regan chose to continue the cabinet councils as the primary policy initiators and to use the Office of Policy Development to establish broad themes from which the cabinet councils would operate.

[51]Dick Kirschten, "Once Again, Cabinet Government's Beauty Lies in Being No More Than Skin Deep," *National Journal*, June 15, 1985, p 1419.
[52]Carolyn R. Thompson, "The Cabinet Member as Policy Entrepreneur," *Administration and Society*, Volume 25, No. 4, February 1994, p 395–409.
[53]One White House staffer described the new orientation in the White House under Regan and Bauer as follows: "Regan's aides were saying the kind of things for which they became famous, 'agenda for the future' and such." Peggy Noonan, *What I Saw At The Revolution: A Political Life in the Reagan Era* (New York: Random House, 1990), p 213.

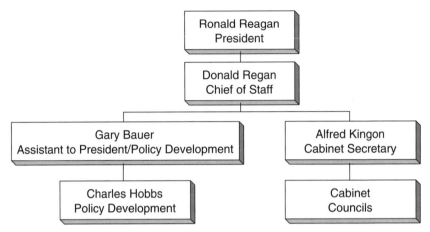

Figure 5.11   Domestic Policy Structure, 1986–1987

Bauer had worked on social issues during the transition and, once the Reagan team had moved into office, had spent a year in the White House under Martin Anderson and Ed Gray. In 1982, he left the Office of Policy Development for a position with the Department of Education as deputy undersecretary of planning, and, in 1985, became the Education Department's liaison to the Economic Policy Council. At Education, Bauer had become a vocal spokesman for conservative values and, when William Bennett was named secretary of Education, Bauer gained a strong supporter for his message.

When Regan brought Bauer to the White House, Bauer had been chairing a task force on the family. Regan, who saw Bauer on television discussing family values, hired Bauer to restore a conservative edge to the White House planning operation (Figure 5.12). Bauer, a staunch supporter of welfare reform because "welfare and poverty are chosen rather than incurred," became the representative for the New Right conservatism in the White House.[54] Within the White House, Bauer began setting a course of broad policy statements designed to restore the administration's credibility with its conservative base. Bauer's primary role was not to interact with the departments in policy making but rather to reassert the president's conservative themes for public consumption. The White House domestic policy operation had entered yet another phase in its often-changing role during the Reagan administration: the voice of the Reagan Revolution.

Bauer's influence in focusing the revolution rapidly became evident as the departments began to move toward a more conservative approach in pol-

[54]John B. Judis, "The Mouse that Roars: Gary Bauer, the New Right Voice in the White House," *The New Republic*, August 3, 1987, p 23.

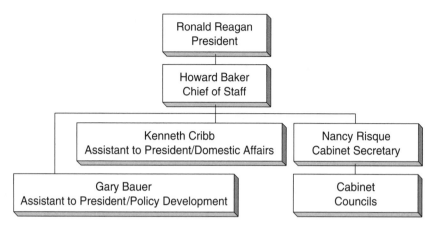

Figure 5.12   Domestic Policy Structure, 1987–1988

icy development. In the Education Department, for example, a task force recommended greater parental involvement in education as one tool to improve the nation's educational system.[55] This was consistent with Reagan's campaign theme that individuals needed to take more responsibility in their own governance and rely less on government technocrats.

To a significant extent, however, agenda setting for domestic policy was being moved to a back burner in the White House as the second term began. The Reagan Revolution had focused on cutting taxes, reducing the number of federal programs and cutting bureaucracy, and cutting regulations on business and industry. Throughout the first term, the administration had moved successfully on all fronts. As the second term moved into operation, the domestic policy office was less concerned with achieving legislative objectives than with reasserting the guiding principles of the conservative movement.

As the White House was refocusing the domestic operation, a series of international issues, simmering for several years, began to boil. Although the domestic agenda had moved forward with often stunning success during the first term, the administration had suffered a number of foreign policy failures. The breakdown of Middle East peace talks in 1982 and the pullout of U.S. troops from Lebanon, after the terrorist attack that left U.S. Marines dead, contributed to the sense that the U.S. had focused too heavily on military issues driven by the Cold War and the Strategic Defense Initiative (SDI). Globally, other issues began to surface, such as the Iran-Iraq war that was

[55]Memo from Nancy Risque to the President, "Report of the Domestic Policy Council Working Group on the Parental Role in Education," January 9, 1989, Box 24, ED 606385, Ronald Reagan Presidential Library, Simi Valley, California.

continuing into its fifth year, and a series of terrorist attacks related to the war provoked public demands for retaliation by the U.S. government. Problems of apartheid in South Africa and a revolution in Nicaragua built on the administration's already mounting problems in the international arena.

Iran *Contra* Redefines the Domestic Agenda

As foreign policy issues in general began to move to the forefront of both Reagan's and Regan's attentions, one major issue surfaced that nearly brought down the administration. The Iran-*Contra* affair, as it was known, involved a guns-for-hostages deal arranged by a junior member of the National Security Council, Lt. Colonel Oliver North. The circuitous operation involved selling arms to Iran in exchange for the release of hostages kidnapped by Iranian extremist groups. The money from the arms sale would be funnelled to a rebel contingency, the *Contras*, in Nicaragua, who opposed the authoritarian regime in power. The covert operation not only ran counter to Reagan's frequently stated opposition to any arms-for-hostages deal, but it also violated the Boland Amendments, which prohibited funding the *Contras*.

Throughout 1986, various White House staff, including Regan, became active in the discussions on the arms deal to Iran. By mid-November 1986, Reagan was forced to acknowledge in a televised "*mea culpa*" address to the nation that there had been secret missions to Iran, but he insisted that no weapons-for-hostages deals had been made. A week later, Meese revealed that the White House had been involved in detailed dealings with Iran and with the *Contras*. Meese placed the blame on staff, not on the president. As a result, Regan became the center of the controversy, as questions arose whether he had briefed Reagan on the illegal activities and had gained Reagan's approval or whether he had operated without the president's knowledge.

The Meese revelation forced Regan to divert all his attention to the growing Iran-*Contra* crisis and to seek ways to protect Reagan from being implicated as a conspirator in the operation as well as to protect himself from being implicated. Regan, who had just returned from the Reykjavik Summit between Gorbachev and Reagan, quickly jumped from summitry to damage control. Domestic policy making became secondary to Regan as he began a constant round of meetings with the national security advisor's staff to assess the involvement of members of the White House staff in the arms sale to Iran and subsequent funding of the *Contra* rebels. The Iran-*Contra* affair had begun to seriously erode public support for the Reagan presidency as public approval dropped from a high of 64% in October, 1986, to a bare 40% four months later.[56]

---

[56]*Newsweek* poll conducted by the Gallup Organization, published in *Newsweek* March 16, 1987, p 20.

By early spring, 1987, Reagan continued to deny any knowledge of the Iran-*Contra* dealings. However, numerous press stories surfaced accusing Regan of either withholding information from Reagan or simply lying to him about the national security staff's actions. As the chief of staff with responsibility for the National Security Council, the argument arose that Regan should have known about the dealings. If he did not know, they argued, he was inadequately managing the White House. If he did know, he was covering up. Although Regan stridently contended that he knew nothing about the initial stages of the plan and little about its operation, Reagan sought his resignation.

In a meeting on February 23, 1987, between the two, Reagan formally asked Regan to resign. Regan sought and was granted a delay in the formal announcement until the Tower Commission Report was released on February 26, which he believed would clear him of any cover-up. Several days later, Reagan phoned Howard Baker, former Senate Majority Leader, and asked him to take over as chief of staff. Baker flew to Washington, D.C., to meet secretly with Reagan. Not unexpectedly, the national media leaked the story. Regan found out about the offer to Baker and immediately resigned effective the next day, February 27.[57] In a terse, one-line letter, Regan said:

> Dear Mr. President:
>   I hereby resign as Chief of Staff
> to the President of the United States.
>
>   Respectfully yours,
> DONALD T. REGAN

Reagan called Regan that afternoon, said he was sorry for the way the situation turned out, and acknowledged that Baker had indeed been asked to take over as chief of staff. Regan immediately left the White House. The two never saw each other again. Regan, bitter about his tenure in the White House, noted that Reagan had not only failed to tell him in person about Baker's imminent move to the White House, but had not even personally written the response to his resignation later. "In my time with President Reagan," Regan noted, "I had seen many such letters, and I knew that someone else had written it for him."[58]

On March 2, Howard Baker, the former senior senator from Tennessee, was formally sworn in as chief of staff and began what was often referred to as "Reagan's third term."[59] Baker entered the White House with the primary responsibility of rebuilding the president's battered public image and restoring support within Congress, support that had been seriously eroded by the effort within the National Security Council to circumvent legislative intent and statutory mandates in dealing with the Nicaraguan *Contras*. Baker,

[57]Donald Regan, *For the Record*, p 374.
[58]Ibid, p 374.
[59]Larry Martz, "The Long Road Back," *Newsweek*, March 16, 1987, p 18.

popular among both Democrats and Republicans, was widely known as a man of unquestioned integrity and uncommon political sense—exactly what Ronald Reagan needed after the disastrous Iran-*Contra* events.[60] Although Reagan had been absolved by the Tower Commission's report of involvement in the Iran-*Contra* dealings, members of the National Security Council staff were found culpable.[61] Baker's activities immediately were focused on public relations activities, much as Gerald Ford's staff had undertaken after Nixon's resignation.

Domestic policy making was subsequently put on the back burner while Baker addressed the primary concerns surrounding Iran-*Contra*. Not only had Ronald Reagan suffered perhaps irreparable harm, but the institution of the presidency had again been rocked by crisis. Baker's task was to restore both Reagan's image and that of the presidency itself.

Baker's strategy was to produce an immediate public relations coup that would focus attention away from Iran-*Contra* and expand on more successful international issues. For Baker, Reagan's principal opportunity for recapturing broad-based political support was to achieve a major arms control agreement with Soviet leader Mikhail Gorbachev. As a senior member of the Senate Foreign Relations Committee, Baker had played a major role in the debates on the Strategic Arms Limitation Talks (SALT II) during the Carter administration. His expertise in arms control and his knowledge of the players in Congress gained while serving as both Senate minority and majority leader provided a strong impetus to move Reagan away from domestic policy to concentrate on east/west relations.

In addition, Baker saw foreign policy as the more successful way to rebuild Reagan's political base in order to ensure that the Republicans did not lose the White House in the 1988 elections. The administration had successfully addressed most of the key issues in the domestic agenda during the first term. Taxes were down, deregulation had been actively pursued in every department and agency, the number of federal programs had been cut (although many were consolidated rather than cut), and numerous programs had been spun off to the states as part of the reemphasis on federalism.

As a result, Baker all but abandoned his interest in the Office of Policy Development. With the domestic agenda successfully implemented during the first term, few key domestic issues remained on Reagan's plate. For Baker, the remainder of the second term should be focused on issues that bridged partisan lines and restored public confidence, which had been severely eroded by Iran-*Contra* in the Reagan presidency.

[60]Martin Anderson, *Revolution*, p 180.
[61]On March 11, 1988, William McFarlane, national security advisor at the height of the Iran-*Contra* affair, pleaded guilty to four federal misdemeanor charges based on evidence that he lied to Congress. Oliver North and John Poindexter, who succeeded McFarlane at the NSC, were subsequently indicted by a federal grand jury.

Baker, however, brought in a new staff, largely at the suggestion of his transition team.[62] Added to the domestic policy team was Kenneth Cribb, a former White House staffer under Anderson and an advocate for conservative social policy, who was given the title Assistant to the President for Domestic Affairs (Figure 5.13). Cribb worked closely with Bauer in moving the conservative agenda forward, each providing new guidance to the departments in policy development. For the first time since Martin Anderson had been at the helm of the domestic policy operation, the White House was urging the departments to move their agendas forward within constraints outlined by the White House. The cabinet councils continued their operations through the Cabinet Affairs Office under Nancy Risque, who had replaced the unpopular Alfred Kingon, but with greater direction from the White House and, in particular, the domestic policy staff.[63]

After less than a year at the helm, Baker returned to his law practice and turned the job over to his deputy, Kenneth Duberstein, who became Reagan's fourth chief of staff. Duberstein continued the course that Baker had charted, which saw the White House domestic policy operations providing clearer direction on the Reagan agenda to the cabinet councils. That agenda became one of conservative social values, focused on rebuilding the family structure to reduce welfare dependence, enhance the educational system, and rebuild economic opportunities.

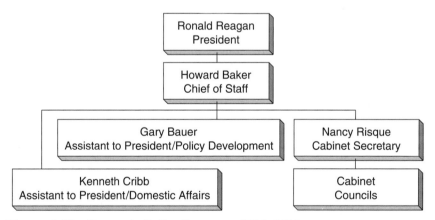

Figure 5.13 Domestic Policy Structure, 1988–1989

[62]Baker's transition team consisted of James Cannon, Ford's domestic policy advisor; Thomas Griscom, Baker's Senate press secretary; and Kenneth Cribb, who had worked under Anderson during the first year of the administration and was widely respected by conservative Republicans. Cribb was added to the original team of Cannon and Griscom by conservatives who were concerned about Baker's moderate leanings.

[63]Ronald Brownstein and Dick Kirschten, "Cabinet Power," *National Journal*, June 28, 1986, p 1582.

Conclusion

Throughout his eight years in office Reagan had four separate domestic policy operations: the first two years under Martin Anderson, the next two years
under Edwin Harper, two years under John Svahn, and finally the last two
years under Gary Bauer and Kenneth Cribb. Anderson had a clear vision of
using the White House domestic policy operation to work with the departments through the cabinet council system to move the Reagan Revolution
forward. For Anderson, that meant tying the domestic agenda to the economic agenda and ensuring that the primary economic issues were cutting
departmental programs as a tool to reduce the budget and gain control over
the burgeoning federal bureaucracy. Anderson and his partner, David Stockman, were extremely successful in their endeavors and kept the departments
focused on the revolution.

Once Anderson left, Harper and Svahn were less successful at managing
the domestic agenda around the themes of the revolution. Departments
began moving in their own directions, which often were at odds with the
administration's broad goals. Not until Gary Bauer and Kenneth Cribb
gained control of the domestic agenda did the White House again move to
focus the departments and constrain departmental initiatives that did not
address the refocused themes of the conservative revolution.

The failure of the domestic policy operation in the White House after
Anderson left can be explained in several ways. Perhaps the best explanation
is that, during the first two years of the administration, Reagan accomplished
his goal of reducing the growth of federal spending and cutting the flow of
federal regulation. Harper and Svahn had fewer items to address and less lee-
way in their policy objectives. The second term was mired in foreign policy
issues, a lack of direction from Regan on domestic issues, and, finally, the
Iran-*Contra* affair, which essentially paralyzed the administration. When
Howard Baker entered the White House in March, 1987, he focused his
attention on rebuilding the image of Reagan and left domestic policy to
Bauer and Cribb, who redefined the role of the domestic policy office within
the themes of the conservative New Right. Duberstein continued the Baker
operation and essentially left Bauer and Cribb alone.

Reagan's departure from office on January 20, 1989, should have set the
stage for George Bush to start with a fresh slate and to continue a proactive
domestic policy process framed within the broad goals of the Reagan Revolution. The Office of Policy Development was positioned to guide the new
administration in those policy goals and to rebuild alliances within the
departments. Bush, however, ignored the Office of Policy Development and
allowed domestic policy to atrophy. This later proved to be his undoing.

Rhetoric overcame substance in the fall campaign as Bush continued to hammer at the issue of patriotism and Dukakis' membership in the ACLU. Typical of the speeches that Bush delivered in the fall was one in San Antonio, Texas, where he said,

> I believe our school children have the right to say the Pledge of Allegiance to the Flag in the United States. I don't know what his problem is with the Pledge of Allegiance. I can't help but feel that his fervent opposition to the pledge is symbolic of an entire attitude that is best summed up in four letters: ACLU.[9]

The environment, education, and the economy moved to second tier status as "flag waving" dominated the campaign. Bush was making major inroads into the base of the Democratic Party, blue-collar workers and first-generation Americans. A bakery worker in New Jersey summed up the view of many voters when he said of Bush, "He's the best man for America. I like the flag. I don't like Jane Fonda, liberals, and communists."[10]

The Campaign Comes to a Close

Few specifics emerged on goals for the broader-based domestic issues. Generic statements became the norm. In a speech at a Colorado high school he pledged to develop a comprehensive program "to invest in our children." Rather than delineate specific proposals, he decried "50 years of liberal programs that did not help children but made them worse."[11]

The environment mirrored education as an issue with little depth of policy. As he stood on the shores of Lake Erie in September, Bush said that, if elected, he would reduce acid rain and speed the clean up of toxic wastes but gave no indication of how the process would proceed. His promises for environmental protection were continually vague as evidenced by what is perhaps the most general statement possible. In the second presidential debate in October, Bush blythly said, "I am an environmentalist. I believe in our parks. I believe in the President's Commission on Outdoors. And I'll do a good job because I am committed."[12]

Education was similarly glossed over with few specifics except for a pledge to increase Reagan's education budget. The economy was given slightly more attention, with broad promises to stimulate the economy with-

---

[9]The issue was framed around a Massachusetts bill that was vetoed by Dukakis that would have required public school children to recite the Pledge of Allegiance in class. See Bill Peterson, "Bush Ran Rhetorical Six Guns in Texas," Washington *Post*, September 26, 1988, p A6.

[10]Maureen Dowd, "Bush, in Reagan Style, Drops Script and Assails Dukakis's Foreign Policy," *New York Times*, September 13, 1988, p D25.

[11]David Hoffman, "Bush Details Child Aid Plan," *Washington Post*, October 6, 1988, p A27.

[12]Transcript of presidential debates, *Washington Post*, October 16, 1988, p A16.

out increasing taxes. "No new taxes" became a campaign pledge, with promises of even reducing taxes for low- and middle-income families.[13]

After two full months of constantly hammering at Dukakis for his liberalism, the Willie Horton incident, and his questionable patriotism, Bush entered election day optimistic about his chances to win the presidency. His decision to focus attention away from more substantive issues and concentrate on the more narrow issues turned out to be the right one. On election day, the voters rejected the Dukakis candidacy and chose George Bush as their president. The Republicans had successfully marshalled their forces again and kept the White House from the opposing party. George Bush had become the first sitting vice president in a century and a half to capture the White House.

The Transition

The transition from a Reagan presidency to a Bush presidency was far easier than the hostile takeovers of recent administrations. It had been sixty years since Republican Calvin Coolidge passed the mantle to Republican Herbert Hoover that a friendly takeover occurred at the White House.

During the election, Ronald Reagan had strongly supported his vice president, criss-crossing the country to stump for the party's nominee. The task of the newly elected administration was to build on the Reagan experiences while still creating new images of leadership. Bush had in his acceptance speech reiterated his commitment to fulfilling the Reagan "mission" but had to establish his own mission. As presidential scholar James Pfiffner aptly noted, "He [Bush] could not be seen to be rejecting his predecessor, yet he had to establish his own administration. He could not throw out loyal Republicans too roughly, yet he had to make his own appointments. He could not change policy directions too sharply, yet he had to set a direction for his own Presidency."[14]

The responsibility for building a Bush presidency fell to transition codirectors Craig Fuller and Robert Teeter, appointed the day after the election.[15] Their task was to build a transition organization focused on creating an agenda for the first 100 days of the administration and on staffing the new administration. That staff entailed 1140 presidential appointments that did not require Senate confirmation, in addition to the 551 cabinet, sub-cabinet, and agency appointments that did require Senate confirmation.

[13]Thomas B. Edsall, "Bush Urges Tax Break on Savings," *Washington Post*, September 18, 1988, p A8.
[14]James Pfiffner, "The Bush Transition", *Presidency Research*, Volume 11, Number 2, Spring 1989, p 22.
[15]The Bush transition team received $3.5 million, an increase from the $2 million Congress provided the 1980 Reagan transition team.

No Clear Objectives

Unlike the Carter and Reagan campaign staffs, however, the Bush campaign staff had given little thought to the transition or to developing the future administration. Campaign staff were directed by Baker to avoid thinking about the future and to steer all of their energies into the November election. Baker's great fear was that any focus on the transition would breed overconfidence, which could then undermine the campaign.[16] Only Chase Untermeyer, a campaign strategist and senior member of the Bush vice presidential office, had done any rudimentary planning for the transition. He had not, however, developed a detailed plan for either a transition organization or transition objectives.

As a result, Fuller and Teeter moved into their transition offices without clear objectives and without specific personnel to manage the various components of the transition. The transition staff however, took shape as the campaign staff became a transition staff (Figure 6.2). Formal titles emerged, and jobs became more clearly defined. Nine offices were subsequently created within the transition team. At the peak of the transition, approximately 125 staff were officially employed in the transition offices, far fewer than the 1500 that Reagan employed at various times during the 1980 transition. Once established, the transition team divided responsibilities into four broad areas: choosing cabinet and sub-cabinet appointments, choosing White House staff, developing packets of information for cabinet officers, and preparing a 100-day plan for the new administration. Fuller and James Baker managed personnel selection for the White House and cabinet while departmental management issues were managed by Pinkerton, Gray, and Untermeyer.

- ♦ Craig Fuller–Codirector
- ♦ Robert Teeter—Codirector
- ♦ James Pinkerton—Policy Director
- ♦ Chase Untermeyer—Personnel
- ♦ C. Boyden Gray—Legal Counsel
- ♦ David Demarest—Public Affairs
- ♦ Janet Mullins—Congressional Relations
- ♦ David Ryder—Operations
- ♦ Thomas Callamore—Liaison with Vice President's Office
- ♦ Fred Fielding—Liaison with Vice President Elect

Figure 6.2   Key Transition Staff, 1988

[16]Fred Barnes, "White House Watch: Job Creation," *The New Republic*, November 21, 1988, p 9.

Departmental management issues centered on groups of transition staff who developed packets of information about the departments for the cabinet nominees. The transition office contacts (or TOCs) for each department prepared reports on the statutory responsibilities of each department, current staffing, and departmental objectives. In large measure, these reports reflected "the notebooks" prepared by the Reagan transition staff for incoming cabinet officers in 1980. The task of the TOCs was not particularly difficult, since Bush was involved in a friendly takeover. Reagan departmental staff provided most of the material needed for the notebooks, requiring few meetings and relatively little research by the transition team. Departmental staff recognized that their assistance with the transition team would be helpful in retaining their jobs.

In addition, the Heritage Foundation was preparing the 900-page *Mandate for Leadership III*, the successor to earlier volumes prepared for each of the two Reagan administrations. *Mandate for Leadership I (1980)* and *Mandate for Leadership II (1984)* provided a department-by-department study of existing and recommended budgets, personnel, and programs for the new administration and was widely used throughout the Reagan years.

Personnel Management

Untermeyer's personnel operation gathered names for the multitude of vacancies that would occur in the departments with the change of administrations. But unlike the Reagan administration that gave the department heads little independence from White House-sponsored personnel, the Bush administration gave the department heads substantial independence in personnel selection. Their argument was that cabinet secretaries want the most qualified people available and actively recruit strong management teams.[17]

Each cabinet secretary was given a list of names by the White House for each senior sub-cabinet, or presidential, appointment. The Bush administration had 312 presidential appointments requiring Senate confirmation. The names provided by Untermeyer were not exclusive and cabinet officers were free to move their own choices into these positions if they were uncomfortable with the White House-generated names.[18] All prospective appoint-

[17]"Politics and Performance: Strengthening the Executive Leadership System," *Task Force Reports to the National Commission on Public Service*, The Volcker Commission Report, Washington, D.C., 1989, p 167. See also James P. Pfiffner, "Nine Enemies and One Ingrate," *The In-and-Outers*, G. Calvin Mackenzie, editor (Baltimore: Johns Hopkins University Press, 1986).

[18]This process followed the October 1988 recommendation of the National Commission on the Public Service, chaired by Elliot Richardson, which said "The President should delegate to department heads the recruitment of noncareer SES and Schedule C appointments within the bounds of general criteria established by the White House. The President should give significant weight to the preferences of the cabinet secretaries in the selection of their immediate subordinates who are presidential appointments."

ments, however, were subject to a White House review, or "scrubbing," process, that ensured compatibility with the Bush agenda.

There were, of course, exceptions to the amount of freedom that cabinet officers were given by the White House. In the case of Jack Kemp at Housing and Urban Development, Untermeyer sent over only one name as a nominee for an assistant secretary position, and Kemp was strongly urged to accept the nominee. He did.

Schedule C appointments, or those at the policy-making but not senior level, were given less independence as the White House sought to move campaign loyalists into the administration. The legion of Bush political supporters was not forgotten during the appointments process. Political supporters who had toiled during the campaign for their candidate were told that their efforts would be rewarded. "We're making sure that those guys who were there when George Bush needed them," said a transition staffer, "know that George Bush is here when they need him."[19] Untermeyer reserved approximately 800 of the 1800 Schedule C jobs for campaign workers and key supporters. As one senior campaign official candidly described the process, "Our people don't have agendas. They have mortgages. They want jobs."[20] The test of loyalty for Bush was not political ideology, as it had been under Reagan, but perseverance and hard work throughout the campaign.[21] Bush was so concerned about ensuring jobs for long-time supporters that he regularly sent Untermeyer notes with 10–20 names that were "must-hires."

The appointment of Lee Atwater, who had directed the campaign for Bush as chairman of the Republican National Committee (RNC), insured that politics would not be ignored in the appointment of departmental staff.[22] Atwater lobbied heavily for appointments for "all of the folks who were living in Iowa for five weeks."[23] Cabinet officers were given lists of names from Untermeyer and Atwater and encouraged, although not mandated as they were under Reagan, to limit their choices to those on the list.

[19]Transition Report, "Campaign Workers Won't Be Ignored When Dividing Spoils," *National Journal*, December 3, 1988, p 3088.
[20]Ann Devroy, "High Level Government Jobs Reserved For Bush Supporters," *Washington Post*, January 14, 1989, p A1. See also Richard Fly, "Help Wanted: 3000 Appointees. Right-Wing Purity Not Required," *Business Week*, January 23, 1989, p 49.
[21]While Untermeyer worked closely with the cabinet officers on filling the presidential appointments, two cabinet secretaries, James Baker and Nicholas Brady, operated without White House oversight. Their personal relationship with Bush guaranteed that all of their nominees would move smoothly through the personnel process.
[22]Following Nixon's reelection in 1972, Bush was tapped as Republican National Committee chairman. Nixon told Bush that the RNC chairman will be "the President's full-time political advisor," attending Cabinet and congressional leadership meetings. The Watergate scandal prevented full development of this plan, but Bush may have designed his relationship with Atwater based on this model.
[23]Transition Report, "Campaign Workers Won't Be Ignored When Dividing Spoils," *National Journal*, December 3, 1988, p 3088.

The list was not a litmus test of philosophical coherence with the president-elect, as it had been under Reagan, but simply represented those who had devoted their time, energies, and financial support to the campaign.

While professional competency and managerial strength were stressed by the president-elect as the basic tenet of departmental jobs, with political activism weighing in as a factor only if competence was ensured, diversity was not overlooked. Taking a leaf from the Carter transition book, the Bush transition team pursued ethnic and gender diversity in their personnel choices. Although it was never considered a priority as it had been under Carter and would become under Clinton, diversity was nevertheless vigorously pursued. Outreach programs were created within the transition team to recruit women, Hispanics, and African Americans into the administration.[24]

When the outreach programs failed to recruit the numbers of people that the transition team was seeking, each of the state Republican political organizations was asked to suggest names. Jesse Jackson, noting the absence of African Americans at the senior levels of the administration, met with Bush to urge a more aggressive approach to diversification. This followed a meeting between Bush and Benjamin Hooks, executive director of the National Association for the Advancement of Colored People (NAACP), who similarly urged greater diversification.

The 100-Day Plan

Development of the 100-day plan was the last issue to be addressed, as the transition team focused on key administration personnel decisions and on the departmental overviews by the TOCs. Perhaps the simple explanation for the delay in the 100-day plan was the absence during the campaign of a clear domestic or foreign policy agenda. With the campaign focused on themes of patriotism and family values and on repeated attacks on Dukakis' liberalism, few specific proposals were drafted. Even the often-promised support for an environmental presidency, an education presidency, and a law-and-order presidency had few substantive objectives for the transition team to build on. James Pinkerton, the point-person for the 100-day plan on the transition team, offered another view on the relatively late focus on agenda setting. His comment was that the new administration simply wasn't ready to move on an agenda since that task should fall to the top policy makers, many of whom had not been chosen. Pinkerton maintained that Bush's agenda would not be developed until the White House was fully staffed. "When the White House is 5% staffed," said Pinkerton, "[we're not ready] to write a 100-day plan."[25]

[24]Judith Havemann, "Bush Names 3 Transition Aides to Help Recruit Blacks, Hispanics and Women," *Washington Post*, November 29, 1988, p A14.
[25]Burt Solomon, "Formulating Policy for Bush In 1989 Is Lagging Behind at Transition Office," *National Journal*, December 17, 1988, p 3207.

As the transition edged on, lobbyists inundated the Bush staff with ideas for policy goals for the new administration. Environmental groups, for example, sent in over 700 proposals for the transition team to review. A coalition of more than thirty organizations developed the *Blueprint on the Environment* and suggested names for senior positions at the Environmental Protection Agency (EPA). Similarly, the Aircraft Owners and Pilots Association, with 275,00 members, offered to work with the transition team on transportation issues and provide names for Transportation secretary, Federal Aviation Administration chief, and National Safety Board chairman. The influence of interest groups in the transition was, in general, and particularly in environmental policy, far more significant in the Bush transition than in any transition in recent history. This was due, quite simply, to the absence of well-developed proposals during the campaign itself.

The transition team aggressively moved into policy development only after Christmas, once key personnel decisions had been made. The policy planning part of the transition was, as it had been throughout the campaign, given minimal attention. As the inauguration grew closer, a string of nightly, three-hour meetings began to take place with John Sununu, Richard Darman, Teeter, Brady, Andrew Card, Roger Porter, and David Demarest. They reviewed Bush's campaign positions and assembled a series of issues they thought might arise soon after they took office. Their goal was only to develop a "discrete number," as one transition staffer described it, of initiatives for the early months of the administration.[26] They were not attempting any long-term planning or planning past the first three months of the administration.

The Sununu group focused their energies on pursuing initiatives that could be achieved within the first 100 days of the administration. The 100-day plan, as it became known, was eventually developed around goals that they felt could be molded into a successful legislative package. The "kinder, gentler" nation that George Bush envisioned allowed the group exceedingly broad discretion in focusing the agenda. Their aim became simply to create policy goals that were achievable, rather than goals that were at the forefront of the campaign or that met long-standing commitments of the president-elect.[27]

The goals that were most likely to achieve legislative success included refining the Clean Air Act, which was due for reauthorization; supporting

---

[26]Burt Solomon, "Bush Promised New Faces But He's Hiring Old Friends," *National Journal*, January 21, 1989, p 143.

[27]As the campaign drew to a close, Bush became reluctant to discuss any specific policy issues. He said in one interview that "I don't want to be dragged" into specific questions about a Bush presidency, such as how he would cut the federal budget or what federal programs he would maintain or reduce. See David Hoffman, "Bush Shuns Specifics in Final Weeks," *Washington Post*, October 16, 1988, p A1.

reductions in the tax rate on capital gains; developing new education pro-grams; and initiating child care programs. Each of these legislative initiatives were in line with the key objectives of the campaign: the environment, the economy, education, and family values.[28] Simpler proposals included creat-ing an ethics advisory panel for the executive branch on a par with the ethics committees in Congress.

Shaping Bush's Foreign Policy

Bush's modest domestic agenda was balanced by an equally modest foreign affairs agenda. As in domestic affairs, significant debate on substantive issues in foreign affairs had been absent. The Bush campaign strategy was to deflect discussion from foreign policy to imply support for the Reagan agenda. Polls consistently indicated that most Americans agreed with Reagan's military build-up and hard-line tactics against the Soviet Union.

However, there were aspects of the Reagan agenda that Bush did want to change and came to light only after the election. In a press conference announcing the appointment of Brent Scowcroft as National Security Advi-sor, Bush made his first major statement about the impending changes in for-eign policy. "I want to have a new look," he said. "We're going to formulate *our* policies."[29] As a result, the transition team focused primarily on military issues, such as those surrounding the continuation of Reagan's strategic defense initiative (SDI), support for the single-warhead mobile Midgetman missle, and the reduction in missile warheads proposed in the Strategic Arms Reduction Treaty (START). Broader foreign policy issues were considered, such as holding a summit with Soviet leader Mikhail Gorbachev and ensuring that the Soviets honor the February 15, 1989 deadline for troop withdrawal from Afghanistan. But in deference to James Baker, who needed time for pol-icy briefings at the State Department, few decisions were agreed on.

Key Appointments: Cabinet and White House Staff

As the transition team was reviewing departmental programs, creating lists for the vast array of presidential appointments, and developing the 100-day plan, Bush focused on the administration's key appointments. Those appoint-ments would set the tone for the new administration, a tone that would, as he said, "give him a new look" and set him apart from Reagan.

---

[28]Burt Solomon, "Low Expectations," *National Journal*, November 12, 1988, p 2841.
[29]Transition Report, "Scowcroft's Views Often At Odds With Those Held by Reagan Team," *National Journal*, December 3, 1988, p 3087.

The new look was a blend of cabinet government and a strong White House staff. Bush placed a small cadre of loyalists in both cabinet and White House positions, allowing him to publicly embrace the merits of a strong cabinet without foregoing policy control through the White House.

Twelve hours after the election, Bush appointed campaign chairman James Baker to head the State Department. Baker's appointment was followed by the nomination of campaign finance chairman Robert Mosbacher to head the Commerce Department and of long-time friend Nicholas Brady who was retained at Treasury. Baker, Mosbacher, and Brady would form the core of the cabinet insiders. The assortment of remaining cabinet offices went to mending political fences (Elizabeth Dole at Labor), building political bridges with Congress (John Tower at Defense), assuaging the conservative right wing of the party (Jack Kemp at Housing and Urban Development and William J. Bennett as drug czar), protecting his base among Reagan loyalists (returning Richard Thornburgh at Justice), and keeping his promise for diversity (Manuel Lujan, Jr., at Interior and Louis Sullivan at Health and Human Services). The strength of the cabinet was neither its ideological consistency nor its agreement on key agenda items but rather its commitment to George Bush and its depth of experience within the federal network. As one commentator noted of the cabinet, "The kinds of people Bush has chosen to staff his Administration are not agenda-setters. They are problem-solvers. Like Bush himself, they offer strong qualifications and considerable experience. But no bold ideas."[30] All of the nominees were either old friends, affiliated with the campaign, or had served with the president-elect in the Nixon, Ford, and Reagan administrations. It was a cabinet with a built-in comfort zone, since everyone at the cabinet table had a close relationship with the new president and many with each other. While political realities had governed the process, Bush had successfully created the public image of cabinet-building that focused on experience, competence, and management expertise. In an interview in late December, Bush declared his commitment to competence rather than ideological or political considerations in choosing his senior officials. "The message I'm trying to send," he said, "is experience."[31] Although he successfully created the image of competence, he also reinforced the void in policy direction within the cabinet. The selection process for the White House staff similarly reflected the absence of ideology or agenda, for it melded the vice presidential staff with an assortment of personal friends, campaign staff, and political insiders.

---

[30]William Schneider, "Symbols, Values May Not Be Enough," *National Journal*, January 28, 1989, p 262.
[31]David Hoffman, "Familiar Faces Chosen to Fill Cabinet Room", December 25, 1988, p A1. See also an interview with *USA Today* in which Bush said "I set a goal for a broad-based Cabinet, experienced people." January 9, 1989, p 11A.

The Sununu Factor

The most surprising appointment was New Hampshire Governor John Sununu as chief of staff, who had orchestrated Bush's primary victory and who had become a spokesman for the conservative right within the campaign. Craig Fuller, who had expected to become chief of staff, was passed over for the job because of his perceived relative youth (37) and inexperience. Bush was counseled to seek a stronger figure for his chief of staff to minimize the perception that Baker would become the "deputy president." The *New York Times* senior political correspondent R. W. Apple, Jr. described the appointment of Sununu as "irrefutable evidence that the President-elect intends to be seen as a hands-on leader of his Administration, with no question of deputy presidency for his old friend, James A. Baker III, as some people had suggested."[32] The suggestion of Baker as deputy president was based both on Baker's key role in the Reagan White House and in the Reagan Cabinet and on a frequent reference to Baker as the deputy candidate. One campaign aide jokingly described the Baker-Bush campaign relationship as follows:

> Teeter serves up the menu, and Baker decides what's on the plate, subject to Bush wanting to eat it.[33]

The emerging White House staff, with all of its disparate roots, bore a striking similarity to the Ford White House staff. Ford tried to unite the Nixon White House staff with his own vice presidential staff and new appointees, such as Donald Rumsfeld and Dick Cheney. The result was total chaos and paralysis in policy development. Only after Ford fired the Nixon staff and gave Rumsfeld and Cheney authority to reassign the remaining staff and redesign the organizational structure was order brought to the White House. For Ford, however, the effort came too late to gain control over policy development and Carter captured the presidency in the 1976 election.

The lessons learned from the Ford experience were not lost on John Sununu who, once in office, moved to gain control of the White House. Sununu broke precedent and named two deputy chiefs of staff, Andrew Card and James Cicconi, and a director of operations, Bonnie Newman, to manage the White House (Figure 6.3). With both Fuller and Teeter (who had been offered but rejected a staff position in the White House) gone, Sununu solidified his authority within the White House. With the exception of senior staff brought in directly by Bush, Sununu reviewed all of the staff brought into the White House.

[32]R. W. Apple, Jr. "Bush, Early On: Very Much Involved," *New York Times*, November 20, 1988, AI.
[33]David Hoffman, "Disciplined Bush Run Follows Baker's Recipe", *Washington Post*, October 4, 1988, p A16.

♦ John Sununu—Chief of Staff
♦ Andrew Card—Deputy Chief of Staff
♦ James Cicconi—Deputy Chief of Staff
♦ Chase Untermeyer—Personnel
♦ C. Boyden Gray—Counsel
♦ Marlin Fitzwater—Press Secretary
♦ Brent Scowcroft—National Security
♦ Roger Porter—Domestic Policy
♦ Bonnie Newman—Operations
♦ Frederick McClure—Congressional Liaison
♦ David Demarest—Communications

Figure 6.3   White House Staff, 1989

Sununu also dramatically restructured the operational lines within the White House. All White House senior staff would report to him, with the exception of Brent Scowcroft who demanded direct access to the president. The senior White House staff was trimmed, with positions such as public liaison and intergovernmental affairs moving to second tier status as deputy assistants to the president rather than assistant to the president. Sununu abandoned any ideas of a spokes-of-the-wheel structure such as Carter originally established or a troika structure such as Reagan originally established. Dealings with the Congress, the cabinet, and all aspects of policy development would be managed through the chief of staff. He reinstated the Legislative Strategy Group, which had been cooperatively run by senior staff in the Reagan White House, under the chief of staff. Not surprisingly, as he sorted through White House operations, Sununu confidently maintained that "he [could] oversee all aspects of White House operations."[34] Vice President Dan Quayle became a nonplayer in the new administration as Sununu consolidated his power.

Creating a Domestic Policy Process

Once the White House organizational structure had been put in place, Bush moved to create mechanisms for addressing domestic and foreign policy within the White House. Foreign policy remained firmly in the hands of the National Security Advisor, Brent Scowcroft, and the National Security Council. Domestic policy fell under the umbrella of "all aspects of White House operations" and was rapidly pulled within Sununu's jurisdiction.

---

[34]Ann Devroy, "Teeter, Citing Family Concerns, Says No to White House Post," *Washington Post*, January 10, 1989 p A4.

This was a divergence from the Reagan model for domestic policy development, in which Ed Meese reported directly to Reagan. Similarly, in the Carter administration, Stuart Eizenstat reported directly to Carter. Under Ford, however, the chief of staff oversaw all policy development. It was the Ford model that Sununu emulated, a model that Roger Porter had operated comfortably within as executive director of Ford's Economic Policy Board.[35]

The domestic policy umbrella under Sununu was divided into two broad areas: White House policy development under Porter, Assistant to the President for Economic and Domestic Policy, and cabinet-initiated policy development under David Q. Bates, Cabinet Secretary.

The Cabinet Secretary: Managing Cabinet Councils

On one side of the domestic policy umbrella was Bates, who became an immediate player in managing the domestic policy process because of his long-standing relationship with Bush. As a long-time friend of Bush's son Jeb, Bates had grown up as part of the Bush household. In 1978, he was hired by Bush to serve as a personal assistant and worked in both the 1980 and 1988 presidential campaigns.

Bates's role as cabinet secretary was to manage the two cabinet councils (Figures 6.4 and 6.5), continued from the Reagan administration, that oversaw cabinet-developed domestic and economic policy. The Domestic Policy Council and the Economic Policy Councils were, according to the May 8, 1989, White House press release, continued in the new administration to advise the president "in the formulation, coordination, and implementation of economic and domestic policy."[36] The membership on the Domestic Pol-

◆ President (Chair)	
◆ Attorney General (Chair Pro Tempore)	◆ President (Chair)
◆ Secretary of the Interior	◆ Secretary of the Treasury
◆ Secretary of HHS	(Chair Pro Tempore)
◆ Secretary of HUD	◆ Secretary of State
◆ Secretary of Transportation	◆ Secretary of Agriculture
◆ Secretary of Energy	◆ Secretary of Labor
◆ Secretary of Education	◆ Trade Representative
◆ Secretary of Veterans Affairs	◆ Council of Economic Advisors

Figure 6.4   Domestic Policy
Council, 1989

Figure 6.5   Economic Policy
Council, 1989

[35]Ford separated economic and domestic policy making in the White House, creating the Economic Policy Board while maintaining the Domestic Council.
[36]"Statement on the Economic and Domestic Policy Councils," May 8, 1989, Presidential Papers.

icy Council was limited to the domestic cabinet officers, with Vice President Quayle, Office of Management and Budget (OMB) director Richard Darman, Environmental Protection Agency administrator William K. Reilly, and John Sununu sitting as ex-officio members. The Economic Policy Council was broadened to include the secretary of State, the Trade Representative, and the chair of the Council of Economic Advisors. Other cabinet members and White House staff could attend cabinet council meetings if they were interested in the issues at hand. The process was intended to facilitate broad debate on policy issues without burdening cabinet members who might not have an interest in those issues.

With relatively few changes, this was the model that Richard Nixon had established in 1970 with the original Domestic Council. Bill Clinton became the first president to significantly change the composition of the cabinet council by adding a host of White House staff to the membership in 1993.

The role of the two cabinet councils was to deal with policy issues that crossed departmental lines that individual cabinet members could not easily deal with. Members of the cabinet councils identified the issues and then pursued solutions that addressed the concerns of each of the departments involved.[37] The lead department on an issue was responsible for the majority of the research and preparation of a draft proposal. That proposal was then discussed and refined by the larger membership before a proposal was sent to the White House. Three professional staff from the cabinet secretary's office were assigned to each of the cabinet councils to manage the process.

However, unlike the Carter administration in which Stu Eizenstat's staff reviewed and commented on the cabinet cluster recommendations, Bates's staff provided primarily research and coordination assistance. The final product, known as a policy option memorandum, then went to Bush without a White House review or recommendation attached to it. Rather, the proposal had at the end a statement such as "The Attorney General supports Option 1; The Secretary of HHS supports Option 2."

Thornburgh's Agenda Setting

The Domestic Policy Council tackled such wide-ranging issues as the repeal of catastrophic health insurance by Congress, support for the death penalty for drug kingpins, medical malpractice reform, white collar crime, minority education, and tort reform. Few of the issues, however, were key agenda items for the administration but rather were issues of concern to specific cabinet members. Many of the issues focused on the Domestic Policy Council chair Richard Thornburgh's own agenda within the Justice Department. Since Thornburgh set the agenda of each council meeting, it was relatively easy to focus the agenda on issues of concern to the Justice Department.

[37]Interview with Richard Thornburgh.

To a significant degree, the narrow focus of the Domestic Policy Council and its failure to address larger issues was due to the absence of a well-articulated domestic agenda in either the campaign or the transition. Cabinet members often spent the council meetings arguing over what the administration's perspective should be on given issues. Few cabinet members had a clear view of where the newly elected president wanted to take the administration since neither the campaign nor the transition had focused the agenda.[38]

When Bush took the chair of the Domestic Policy Council meetings, he encouraged debate over policy issues.[39] Rather than provide direction to the council or narrow the options he wanted considered, he allowed wide-ranging debate to proceed.[40] The result was a policy structure that was primarily reactive rather than proactive, seeking to engineer routine policy issues that required inter-departmental management.

Marching Orders

As the inauguration grew closer, numerous opportunities arose for the president-elect to provide policy direction to the leaders of the new administration. But Bush rejected these opportunities and continued to abdicate his role as the pacesetter for the emerging agenda. In early January, Bush was asked in an interview by *USA Today*, "What will you tell your Cabinet?" His answer was "We'll outline my priorities. We'll just spell it all out on how I want to see them work with Congress, how we'll work with each other, how I'd like to emphasize the very seriousness of the conflict-of-interest, ethical stank I talked about during the campaign. I'll talk to these teammates of mine."[41] Two days later he met with the cabinet designees as they assembled at Blair House for a private cabinet meeting. Although the opportunity was there to clarify presidential goals, Bush offered little guidance for departmental agenda setting. Rather than provide strong and clear guidance on the objectives of the administration and the direction he wanted his departments to take, Bush read off a list of "marching orders" that he took out of his pocket and read to the group. They were repeated after the inauguration at a swearing-in ceremony for White House staff.

Marching Orders for the Cabinet
- Think big
- Challenge the system

[38]Thornburgh argued that the Domestic Policy Council "reacted to policy issues" as they arose and did not formulate policy. Interview with Thornburgh.

[39]The Domestic Policy Council met approximately once every five weeks, with the working groups from the departments meeting approximately every week.

[40]Interview with Richard Thornburgh. Supported in interview with Andrew Card.

[41]Interview with the president-elect, *USA Today*, January 9, 1989, p 11A.

- Don't write kiss-and-tell books
- Don't leak
- Support the President no matter what your view
- Work with Congress
- Represent the United States with dignity
- Adhere to the highest ethical standards[42]

The marching orders covered no policy goals for the administration, nor did they provide guidance on policy development. Cabinet officers felt free to pursue any policy issues that they wanted within the Domestic Policy Council as long as they fell within the broad rubric of the conservative agenda initiated during the Reagan administration. Since Bush had been elected largely to continue the Reagan mandate of 1980, cabinet officers were comfortable delving into issues with little White House guidance. But the absence of White House guidance did not seriously affect policy development, since most cabinet appointments were focused on enhancing departmental management. Bush had carefully chosen a cabinet whose credentials were primarily as managers rather than activists.

The principle obstacle to policy initiation, however, was not the White House but the Office of Management and Budget, with its constant oversight of departmental spending. OMB under the strong hand of Richard Darman was aggressively cutting departmental spending as a prerequisite to deficit reduction. As a result, initiatives moved through the Domestic Policy Council were aimed at reforming not creating programs. For many programs that the council discussed, *reforming* was a euphemism for *reducing* or *cutting*.

Darman and Sununu built a tight web around the policy process by controlling the president's budget process. Their shared commitment to fiscal conservatism ensured that policy initiatives with new costs attached were shelved and that departmental budget proposals were focused on reducing programmatic costs.

Roger Porter: Micromanaging the Domestic Agenda

Under the other half of the domestic policy umbrella was Roger Porter, the Assistant to the President for Economic and Domestic Policy, whose job was to create a broad domestic agenda from which the departments could focus individual initiatives.[43] While the Cabinet Councils were arguing among themselves on policy direction, Porter's office was trying to provide that very policy direction.

[42]David Hoffman, "Watkins, Bennett Named to Cabinet; Bush Orders New Team to Think Big, Avoid Kiss and Tell Books", *Washington Post*, January 13, 1989, p A16.
[43]Porter had played tennis with Bush while both were serving in the Ford White House. Bush asked Porter to leave his position at the Kennedy School of Government at Harvard to assume control of the domestic policy operation in the White House.

Porter had taken the job with the requirement that his title include the words "economic and domestic policy," a requirement designed to ensure a unified approach to the administration's economic and domestic policy development. Presidents Ford and Carter had created separate economic policy units, which had often been at odds with the domestic policy units. The Reagan White House had merged the two operations and produced a more effective policy process.

Porter's demand for the dual title was also a power play within the White House ranks to ensure that Bates' twin cabinet councils could not control more policy issues than Porter's operation. Porter, who had worked on both the Ford and Reagan White House staffs in policy development, was leery of Bates and his nearly total inexperience in policy management.[44] Porter was merely trying to level the playing field as much as he could as he brought both economic and domestic policy into his west wing office. As the administration moved into full gear, Porter's initial concerns over Bates proved well founded as they started to clash over who controlled certain policy areas. White House deputy chief of staff Andrew Card noted, "There was a disconnection between Porter and Bates and major turf battles."[45] Cabinet Affairs and the Office of Policy Development rarely agreed on which office would control policy issues.

As Porter sought to consolidate his influence within the policy development process, he divided his own office into two units: the Office of Policy Development, under William Roper, which managed short-term policy development and the Office of Policy Planning, under James Pinkerton, which managed long-range planning (Figure 6.6). The division allowed Porter to create two policy units and build credibility as the president's primary policy advisor on two separate planes: current and longer-term policy matters. This effectively gave Porter a broader role in policy development than Bates and ensured that Porter's operation would be involved in a wider range of discussions with Bush than the more narrowly focused firefighting issues that the Domestic Policy Council was generally involved with.

Porter's Domestic Policy Structure

Porter's staff began to work directly with the departments to review existing programs to ensure, as one OPD staff member described, "that the President's interests, goals, and policies are served on a daily basis, and monitored and that people are reined in even though you're all ideally on the same team."[46]

---

[44]Porter was staff director to the Economic Policy Board in the Ford Administration and Director of the White House Office of Policy Development in the Reagan Administration. In addition, he was executive secretary of the Cabinet Council on Economic Policy under Reagan.
[45]Interview with Card.
[46]Interview with Rae Nelson.

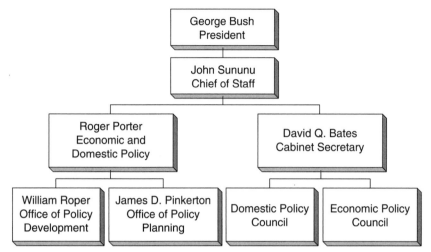

Figure 6.6   Domestic Affairs, 1989

The Office of Policy Development began working closely with the departments to focus departmental goals on the broad themes of the administration, particularly stream-lining programs where possible to reduce spending.

Roper, a pediatrician who had held a White House fellowship in 1982–1983 in the Reagan White House, was brought in by Porter.[47] Pinkerton moved into the White House job through his work on both the campaign and the transition team.[48]

Pinkerton's operation, which was the larger of the two policy units, included twenty-one staff with three associate directors, one deputy associate director, and one director of administration. The policy operation was divided into seven broad categories:

1. domestic economic policy
2. international economic policy
3. environment
4. energy
5. natural resources policy
6. health and human services
7. administration

[47]Roper remained at the White House after his fellowship ended in 1983 until 1986, when he became administrator of the Health and Human Services Department's Health Care Financing Administration, which runs Medicare and Medicaid.

[48]Pinkerton worked in the Reagan White House and in 1985 moved over to the vice president's political action committee and then to the presidential campaign.

By the end of November 1989 two more policy areas were added, reflecting the increasing role in policy management that the Office of Policy Development was beginning to play:

8. education, housing, urban development
9. transportation policy and legal policy

Although Porter had carefully structured his office to be the dominant player in policy development, few major initiatives arose from either the Office of Policy Development (OPD) or the Office of Policy Planning (OPP) during the course of the administration. The OPD became bogged down in working out programmatic details and building consensus within the departments on policy proposals rather than providing broad policy guidance.[49]

Porter as Honest Broker

The concept of consensus building permeated the OPD. Roper, who had maintained a strong relationship with Porter after leaving the White House in 1983, built the OPD around principles established by Porter. Those principles entailed a policy process built on the politics of inclusion. For Porter, policy making had to ensure not only consensus among the players, but also to ensure that the policy process did not exclude any of the departments that would be affected by a change in policy direction. This meant, according to Porter, involving broad participation by the cabinet, departments and agencies, White House staff and other components of the Executive Office of the President, such as the OMB and CEA. The result was a cumbersome, time-consuming process that placed the White House staff in a coordinating rather than agenda-setting role. This was in line with Porter's view that the White House staff should maintain its role as "honest brokers" and not policy initiators.[50]

Similarly, the OPP failed to emerge as the center of policy development. According to Pinkerton, however, the failure of OPP to move into a major policy role was due not to an absence of effort by his staff but rather to an absence of support from more senior staff. He unabashedly described his tenure in the White House in an article for the *New Republic* as "Life in Bush Hell."[51] Pinkerton argued that while Bush urged a "kinder, gentler nation," he provided little support to his own staff for specific policies that would implement that goal. Roger Porter was not eager to set the agenda for Bush,

[49]Interview with Rae Nelson.
[50]Roger Porter, *Presidential Decision Making* (Baltimore, Maryland: Johns Hopkins University Press, 1982).
[51]James Pinkerton, "Life in Bush Hell," *The New Republic*, December 14, 1992, p 22.

noting that "Nobody elected me to make policy. I'm here to provide my best advice."[52] Porter saw his role in the administration as one of an honest broker who did not establish policy or even provide recommendations on policy, but rather ensured that Bush was presented a wide variety of options. Porter described himself as an "honest broker who has the responsibility for looking at the problem from the vantage point of the president and making sure that the options developed are optimal from the standpoint of the president."[53]

Pinkerton: Domestic Policy Loose Cannons

Pinkerton subsequently embarked on his own agenda setting for the administration, developing proposals for "The New Paradigm," which argued for new strategies for empowering citizens on their own behalf. The core idea of Pinkerton's empowerment strategy was to provide options for people receiving social services rather than mandating which services they were to use. For example, Pinkerton encouraged school choice, in which vouchers would allow students to attend either public or private schools. Vouchers would allow renters of subsidized housing to go into the suburbs rather than rely on public housing.[54] The concepts underlying empowerment were more radical than either Bush or his key advisors were willing to advocate, for they assumed a radical restructuring of government's relationship to its citizens. As one observer noted, "It's dubious to think that George Herbert Walker Bush is going to be the Eldridge Cleaver of the 1990's."[55]

But no one stopped Pinkerton, and he continued to write memos and give speeches on the importance of empowering the individual to release him/her from dependence on government programs. Sununu went so far as to approve an Empowerment Task Force, but it never succeeded at building broad coalitions of support either within or without of the White House.

As Pinkerton was increasingly moved to the rear of the policy-making structure, he nevertheless continued to float long-range policy ideas within the White House. Not surprisingly, few of his ideas were moved forward as the White House focused its energies on the short-term problems of budget cutting and taxes. Pinkerton's frustration mounted as he pushed Porter and Sununu to establish a framework for long-range planning within which the OPP could work. "People got tired," he said, "of hearing me sputter: We have to have a plan. This is my plan. If you hate my plan, fine. But what's

[52]Michael McQueen, "Presidential Policy Adviser Faces Complaints That His Idea Menu Offers Leftovers and No Punch," *Wall Street Journal*, June 20, 1989, p A20.
[53]Pat Bodnar, "The President's Honest Broker," *The Christian Science Monitor*, September 6, 1989, p B1.
[54]Burt Solomon, "Power to the People?", *National Journal*, January 26, 1991, p 206.
[55]Op cit.

your plan?"[56] Pinkerton never received a satisfactory answer but continued to encourage longer-range thinking within the upper echelons of the White House.

After nearly two years in the White House, William Roper left and was replaced by Charles Kolb as director of the Office of Policy Development (Figure 6.7). Kolb, who wrote a scathing book on the ineptitude of the domestic policy operation, painted a picture of a complete failure by the White House to set an agenda for the administration and to rein in the departments.[57]

Porter Focuses on Core Issues

While Roper and Pinkerton operated within their own limited spheres, Porter concentrated his energies on what he considered to be the core issues that the president had to address. He was particularly concerned with several major bills in Congress, notably the Clean Air Act and the Civil Rights Act. Both acts carried provisions that Bush considered to be inordinate restraints on business. His goal was to reduce federal mandates and therefore reduce business costs to stimulate the sagging economy.

Since Bush hoped to reorient each of these pieces of legislation within a less-constrictive framework, Porter directed his energies at reviewing every action that Congress took to rewrite the legislation. He met constantly with House and Senate committee members to rewrite various parts of the legislation and rallied constituent groups to support the president's point of view. As he had with the operations of OPD, Porter sought to bring numerous actors with a vested interest into the discussions and to build a consensus among those actors for the president's position. Although he was often accused of micromanaging the issues, he nonetheless did what he set out to do. For Porter, the process of building consensus was slow, arduous, painstaking, and usually successful.

Moving the Process at a Faster Clip

The domestic policy process that Porter created in the White House met the objectives that Porter had established: slowly build consensus and weave policy proposals that satisfy broad constituencies. It was a process called *multiple advocacy*, a term he coined to describe the policy process in the Ford Economic Policy Board and that he supported throughout his tenure in the Bush administration.[58]

[56]Ibid, p 27.
[57]Charles Kolb, *White House Daze: The Unmaking of Domestic Policy in the Bush Years* (New York: The Free Press, 1994).
[58]See Roger Porter's *Presidential Decision Making* (1982) for a discussion of multiple advocacy.

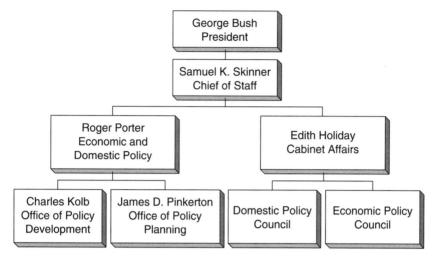

Figure 6.7 Domestic Affairs, 1991

Since the administration lacked a domestic agenda when it entered office, Porter saw his role as developing that agenda around the core themes of the campaign: reductions in federal spending, crime, education, drugs, and the environment. This entailed the time-consuming process of nurturing creation of new policies within the departments and building the coalitions of support necessary to move those policies through the legislative process.

Throughout the first year of the administration, few policy initiatives emerged. The administration backed away from its support for reducing capital gains taxes, which had been loudly touted during the campaign; vacillated on a position on imposing a fee on depositors to provide new funds for the federal deposit insurance corporation, which had been bailing out the faltering savings and loan industry; and failed to take a clear stand on the move to repeal catastrophic health insurance. The strongest positions were vetoes of legislation to raise the minimum wage and to expand abortion rights. Bush "is like a captain of a ship who can read longitude and latitude," was one description, "but doesn't know where his port or destination is."[59]

There were also failures by the White House to coordinate with the departments on policy issues that were being debated in Congress. During the debate in the House over an amendment on the use of cleaner auto fuels, Environmental Protection Agency Director William K. Reilly told one subcommittee that he opposed the amendment while John Sununu told another subcommittee that the administration was neutral on the amendment. In a

[59]Janet Hook and Chuck Alston, "Mixed Signals, Agenda Gap Plague Bush's First Year," *Congressional Quarterly*, November 4, 1989, p 2921.

similar failure of policy coordination, some White House staff were supporting the repeal of catastrophic health care while Health and Human Services
Secretary Louis Sullivan was supporting retention of key elements of the
program. And Housing and Urban Development Secretary Jack Kemp
endorsed raising the ceiling on federal guarantees for mortgages when the
White House was opposing it.

By the end of the first year in office, the administration was being given
low marks for its handling of domestic policy. Not only had it failed to provide clear direction to the departments in policy matters, but it had failed to
develop any major legislative initiatives during the first year. Most debates in
Congress focused on presidential responses to existing legislation rather than
presidentially initiated legislation. "The president hasn't challenged Congress to do anything," contended James Sundquist of the Brookings Institution.[60] Sundquist's nonpartisan view was shared by the clearly partisan view
of Democratic leader Dan Rostenkowski (D-Illinois), who said of Bush,
"He's not headed for greatness."[61]

The Clean Air Act: The Cornerstone of Domestic Policy

As the cabinet councils, the Office of Policy Development, and the Office of
Policy Planning were working on policy strategies, Roger Porter was devot-
ing his energies to the extension of the 1977 Clean Air Act (PL 95-95). The
law was enacted in 1970 and amended significantly in 1977. The core of the
law required states to enact pollution controls that met federal air quality
standards to protect public health. But, by 1990, most urban areas had been
unable to meet the strict guidelines established by the Environmental Protection Agency under the 1977 amendments.

The debate in Congress centered on how stringent the new law should
be in mandating new standards for clean air. Environmentalists argued that
avoiding imposing additional requirements to limit air toxins would lead to
additional cancers, neurological disorders, and significant public health problems. In addition, the earth's ecological system was being damaged and the
food chain irreparably altered. Business and industry leaders, particularly
from the industrial midwest and northeast, argued that the cost of removing
hazardous pollutants from the air had a substantial price in lost jobs and
increased costs that consumers were unwilling to pay.

During the previous eight years, the Reagan administration and Senate
majority leader Robert Byrd (D-W Va) had effectively blocked any overhaul
of the Clean Air Act. Byrd discouraged action on the bill for fear that changes

---

[60]Janet Hook and Chuck Alston, "Mixed Signals, Agenda Gap Plague Bush's First Year,"
Congressional Quarterly, November 4, 1989, p 2926.
[61]Op cit.

would reduce the market for the high-sulphur coal mined in West Virginia. But the increasing concerns over the ozone layer and the problems of global warming convinced the Democrats in Congress that revisions in the law were necessary, and they began an aggressive move to rewrite the act. Led by the newly elected Senate majority leader George Mitchell (D-Maine) who replaced Byrd in 1989, the Senate rewrote the legislation to reduce smog, acid rain, and toxic air pollution.

Bush was forced to take an active role in the massive changes being written into the Clean Air Act, a role in which Roger Porter became the key player. Porter moved to build a consensus among the major players on a bill that would satisfy the Bush administration. Porter assembled staff from the Energy Department, Office of Management and Budget, Environmental Protection Agency, and the White House to discuss the costs and benefits of the proposals crafted in the Senate. The constant meetings in Porter's White House office led one staffer to note of the agency envoys, "These people spend so much time here, they just make themselves at home."[62] He then worked assiduously with Congressional leaders to bargain common ground.

The bill that was signed into law was the product of Porter's considerable efforts on behalf of the administration. Without the exhaustive work and numerous meetings by Porter and his staff, the Clean Air Act may never have moved forward or may easily have been vetoed as unacceptable to the White House. But the inordinate amount of time that Porter personally devoted to the Clean Air Act reduced the amount of time he had for other major policy proposals. As he withdrew into the labyrinth of problems with the Clean Air Act, and later the Civil Rights Act, the myriad of other policy issues fell by the wayside. White House staff within the Office of Policy Development became reactive rather than proactive due to Porter's limited guidance on broader issues.

Porter's lack of guidance for his own staff was mirrored by the lack of guidance from either Sununu or Bush to Porter. Their focus was to keep the budget under control, cut the deficit, and discourage new programs. Darman, with the complete support of Sununu, aggressively attacked any new programmatic spending and urged departments to scrutinize every program for ways to reduce spending. With Sununu and Darman leading the charge for budget-cutting, and focusing all of their energies on budget-cutting, the Office of Policy Development staff fell in line by working with the departments to streamline their operations. Porter tried to carve his own niche by mediating legislative conflicts using the same strategy of consensus building and the politics of inclusion that he had nurtured within White House-cabinet relations.

---

[62]Burt Solomon, "A Day in the Life", *National Journal*, July 7, 1990, p 1652.

Foreign Policy Dominates the Bush Agenda

While Sununu and Darman were focused on capping domestic initiatives, Bush was immersed in a host of major foreign policy crises that dominated his time. Fortuitously, this allowed Bush to distance himself from the budget-slashing activities of his two senior advisors and divert the nation's attention to the more ominous problems of world peace. Issues of domestic policy paled as the nation united behind George Bush and his military support for the small nation of Kuwait and its ouster of General Manuel Noriega by force in Panama (Figure 6.8).

In August, 1990, Iraq invaded Kuwait, declaring the small desert nation to be a province of Iraq. The news media carried chilling pictures of brutal attacks on Kuwaiti citizens by Iraqi soldiers, including children murdered in their beds. The United States response was to send 500,000 troops to the Middle East and to mobilize an international coalition of troops to restore the sovereignty of Kuwait.

After months of negotiations with Iraq and warnings that the international and United States forces would attack unless Iraq withdrew from Kuwait, the United States and its allies began to move against the Iraqi troops in Kuwait on January 17, 1991. The war lasted only weeks, with the final truce with a defeated Iraq on February 18, 1991.

The war had captured the nation's attention and brought Bush the highest public opinion ratings of his presidency, with a nearly 90% approval rating. This followed on the footsteps of another major military undertaking in Panama in December, 1989, and January, 1990. Bush ordered troops into Panama to capture its de facto leader, General Manuel Noriega, who was considered one of Latin America's major drug dealers. The attack on Noriega was portrayed by the administration as essential to its policy of stopping the

♦ October 1989: Aborted coup attempt against Manuel Noriega
♦ December, 1989–January 3, 1990: Invasion of Panama and surrender of Noriega
♦ Summer, 1990: Build-up of Iraqi troops on Kuwaiti border
♦ August 1, 1990: Bush publicly calls for "the immediate and unconditional withdrawal of all Iraqi forces"
♦ August 2, 1990: Iraq invades Kuwait
♦ August 8, 1990: Beginning of troop deployment (defensive purposes only)
♦ August 25, 1990: United Nations Security Council votes to use force
♦ November 8, 1990: Bush announces "increase in size of U.S. forces committed to Operation Desert Shield"
♦ January 17–February 28, 1991: War in the Persian Gulf

Figure 6.8   Foreign Policy Initiatives

import of drugs into the United States and to its policy of promoting democracy within our own sphere of influence.

The fall of the Berlin Wall in November, 1989, and the reunification of Germany in October, 1990, the Romanian revolution in December, 1989, that left President Nicolae Ceausescu and thousands of others dead, the August, 1991, coup against Mikhail Gorbachev and the ultimate collapse of the Soviet Union in December, 1991, and the horrors of the Somalian famine throughout 1992 provided ample opportunity for Bush to focus public attention away from the domestic agenda.

A Return to the Domestic Agenda

As the 1992 presidential election grew closer, Bush began to refocus his energies on the domestic agenda. Although he had built a sound record managing foreign policy, his domestic policy achievements were few and far between. In November, 1991, Bush began to meet regularly at 9:15 A.M. on Tuesdays, Wednesdays, and Thursdays for 45 minutes with Sununu, Darman, and Porter to discuss domestic policy issues. With the budget battles behind them, the White House needed to build a package of strong domestic policy initiatives.

The process of restructuring and rebuilding the domestic agenda led to a major overhaul of the domestic policy process in the White House and a shakeup of senior staff. The first casualty of the domestic policy overhaul was chief of staff John Sununu, who reluctantly resigned on December 3, 1991.[63] Sununu, who had been unrelentingly attacked by the media, members of Congress, and a host of others, was caught using government cars to drive to personal events (e.g., a stamp auction, a dentist appointment, his children's school). While the actions were less than egregious, he appeared to violate the strict ethics rules established by the White House for its staff. These rules also applied to the broader federal government, but White House staff were held up as the models for prudence in their activities.

His fall from power was shaped by his own arrogance and badgering of not only White House staff but members of the cabinet and Congress. One of the frequently told stories about Sununu's arrogance involved the meeting he was chairing in the Roosevelt Room of the White House. When Vice President Dan Quayle entered the room and sat down, Sununu continued to talk for half an hour before acknowledging the vice president's presence. Sununu's insistence on being the dominant player in every situation bruised many egos in Washington. Sununu also ruffled numerous feathers in Con-

[63]Sununu's resignation was effective December 15, 1991. Bush, in accepting his letter of resignation, asked him to remain at the White House as Counsellor to the President until March 1, 1992. Sununu agreed to do so.

gress, particularly throughout the budget battles. After Trent Lott unsuccessfully opposed Sununu on the budget, Sununu went in front of the national news media and snapped, "Senator Lott has become an insignificant figure in this process."[64]

Skinner Takes the Reins

Sununu was replaced by Transportation Secretary Samuel Skinner, who had built a strong reputation as a Bush loyalist and a skillful manager (Figure 6.9). Although Skinner had never been part of the Bush inner circle, he had gained broad support within the administration for his handling of the *Valdez* oil spill in Alaska, the San Francisco earthquake, ending the national railroad strike, and developing a national transportation strategy. Skinner had gained his transportation expertise while serving as chairman of the Regional Transportation Authority of Northeastern Illinois, as an appointee of Governor James Thompson. He later gained prominence in national Republican circles as the Illinois director for Bush's presidential campaign in both 1980 and 1988.

Within days after taking over the reins of the White House, Skinner moved to redesign the domestic policy operation. His task was to rebuild the president's sagging image in domestic policy as the Scowcroft, Baker, and Cheney team had in foreign policy. His first move was to build his own domestic policy team. Andrew Card, Sununu's chief deputy, was moved to Skinner's former position as secretary of Transportation. Henson Moore, a former six-term Republican House member from Louisiana and deputy sec-

♦ Samuel K. Skinner—Chief of Staff
♦ W. Henson Moore—Deputy Chief of Staff
♦ Clayton Yeutter—Counsellor to the President for Domestic Policy
♦ C. Boyden Bray—Counsel
♦ Marlin Fitzwater—Press Secretary
♦ Edith Holiday—Cabinet Secretary
♦ Brent Scowcroft—National Security Advisor
♦ Roger Porter—Assistant to the President for Economic and Domestic Policy
♦ Timothy J. McBride—Operations
♦ Nicholas E. Calio—Legislative Affairs
♦ David Demarest—Communications
♦ Constance Horner—Personnel

Figure 6.9   White House Staff, 1992

[64]Eleanor Randolph, "The Washington Chain Saw Massacre," *Washington Post Magazine*, December 2, 1990, p 16.

retary of Energy, was brought in as the deputy chief of staff. Moore in turn replaced a host of lower-level staff.

Perhaps most significant to the new design of domestic policy was the addition of Clayton Yeutter in the newly created position of Counsellor to the President for Domestic Policy in early February, 1992.[65] Yeutter was charged with managing economic and domestic policy for the president, relegating both Porter and Ede Holiday, who had taken over David Bates's job as cabinet secretary, to a lower tier on the policy ladder. To add insult to injury, Yeutter took over Porter's paneled, west-wing corner office.

Skinner charged Yeutter with developing a process to encourage new domestic initiatives for the administration that could be showcased before the election. Asked what specific initiatives he wanted to see, Skinner replied pragmatically, "Any kind. You know, domestic initiatives. I mean, if in fact we need to change the way things are done, we want to improve the system, you gotta have initiatives."[66]

Yeutter's Reign in the West Wing

Yeutter's task in the White House was to create a coherent vision for the domestic agenda and to develop key initiatives within that agenda. He insisted upon and received authority to restructure the policy-making mechanisms within the White House. He abolished both cabinet councils and established the Policy Coordinating Group (PCG) as its replacement. Treasury Secretary Nicholas Brady, who headed the Economic Policy Council, fought the change but was ultimately convinced by Skinner to accept Yeutter's concept. Attorney General William Barr, who had replaced Richard Thornburgh at the Justice Department, had no objections to abolishing the Domestic Policy Council, which had been frequently referred to as "moribund" throughout the administration. Brady, however, successfully convinced Skinner and Yeutter to maintain the Economic Policy Council as a working group within the Policy Coordinating Group, although it would be given the new title, the working group on economic policy.

Skinner, Yeutter and Moore began meeting daily at 7:00 A.M. to develop strategies for domestic initiatives. At 5:30 P.M. each day, they then met with the Congressional liaison team to pursue strategies for moving domestic programs through Congress. Skinner referred to the latter group as the legislative strategy group, reminiscent of the Reagan administration.

The Policy Coordinating Group (PCG) became the principal tool for developing policy initiatives. But unlike the cabinet councils that created

[65]Yeutter left the Department of Agriculture in January, 1991 to head the Republican National Committee (RNC). Yeutter replaced Lee Atwater, who died of a brain tumor. Yeutter was, in turn, replaced by Richard Bond, a former RNC deputy chairman.
[66]Burt Solomon, "Send in the Clones," *National Journal*, March 21, 1992, p 680.

their own agenda items, Yeutter developed the issues around which the agendas would focus. The White House prepared guidelines for the operation of the PCG, noting that:

1. *Meetings and Agendas*
   The PCG will meet as frequently as is necessary to consider issues that merit presidential and cabinet level attention. The Counsellor to the President for Domestic Policy will develop the agendas for these meetings.

   The President will chair meetings of the Policy Coordinating Group. In the President's absence, the Counsellor to the President for Domestic Policy will chair the meetings.

   The PCG Executive Secretary will have responsibility for distributing notices of the meetings and papers that will be considered at the meetings.

2. *Attendance*
   Policy Coordinating Group meetings will include those cabinet officers and other officials with a legitimate interest in the issues under consideration.

   The Counsellor to the President for Domestic Policy, in consultation with the PCG Executive Committee, will extend invitations to PCG meetings.[67]

In large part, the PCG modelled itself after the Carter-developed cabinet cluster process, in which the president's domestic policy advisor, Stuart Eizenstat, assembled groups of cabinet officers to discuss policy issues. Eizenstat identified the issue to be discussed and brought together a small group of cabinet officers with a vested interest in the policy discussion. As had Eizenstat, Yeutter decided which issues would be addressed and which members of the cabinet would be included in the discussion.

But Skinner's operating style had antagonized senior staff. Senior staff, who were never quite sure whether their jobs were secure, were cut from staff meetings almost immediately. The twenty-five senior staff who regularly met with Sununu were excluded from the daily staff meetings in favor of a smaller group of ten, mostly Skinner, appointees. When Skinner indicated that he wanted to remove many top White House staff, Bush personally intervened to protect them.

Skinner's problems with staff were compounded with the appointment of Clayton Yeutter to manage domestic policy. Yeutter's appointment was seen

[67]The White House, "Policy Coordinating Group," February 26, 1992.

by senior staff as an effort to put another management layer between them and the president and as an attempt by Skinner to reduce their influence.

Skinner's Domestic Deterioration

Skinner's failure to establish a workable domestic policy process in the White House and to mitigate staff unrest was compounded by his failure to provide Bush with appropriate political advice. One of the primary roles of the White House staff had been to quickly respond to crisis events, a response that has become known as "firefighting" in the White House. One of Skinner's earliest mishaps was his inability to manage the Los Angeles riots after the Rodney King verdict in May of 1992. In the hours after the riots began in Los Angeles, Skinner's staff provided no clear direction to the president. The debate emerged between OMB Director Richard Darman, who argued that Bush should take a hard law-and-order stand, and HUD Secretary Jack Kemp, who argued for a personal appeal for less violence.

Skinner eventually sided with Darman, a position that led to broad condemnation by the African American community. In an election year, any divisive action by the White House was tactically unwise. Skinner's decision to pursue a strategy of attack on the rioters rather than urging reconciliation was the first of several major miscalculations that eroded his support within the Bush inner circle. Marlin Fitzwater was among the White House staff who strongly urged Bush to pursue a different tactic that focused on compassion for the victims of the riots.

One of the White House speechwriters, Anthony Snow, went even further by arguing for Bush to seize the moment and issue a major speech on racial problems in the United States. David Demarest, Assistant to the President for Communications, also argued for a major speech that would heal rather than castigate.

As the spring of 1992 became the summer of 1992, Skinner's influence with Bush had rapidly dropped. Few policy initiatives had moved forward and Yeutter had been unable to develop a clear agenda for the floundering administration.

By the end of August, 1992, Bush realized the need for yet another change in White House leadership and appointed James Baker chief of staff. Skinner moved to the position of Counsellor to the President. Soon after Baker's arrival, however, both Skinner and Yeutter resigned. The White House staff's dislike for Skinner was evident in a joke passed around the White House. Skinner's resignation was accompanied by a statement that he was returning to Chicago, where he had previously served as U.S. Attorney, to assume the $500,000-a-year presidency of Commonwealth Edison. Staffers began circulating memos with mock urgency advising anyone who owned Commonwealth Edison stock to "sell short, for God's sake, sell short!"

Baker Moves In

Baker immediately began to refocus public attention away from foreign policy toward a revitalized domestic agenda, promising that "President Bush targets America."[68] Baker replaced Skinner's staff with top staff from the State Department, including Robert Zoellick, Under Secretary for Economic and Agricultural Affairs, who replaced Henson Moore as deputy chief of staff; Dennis Ross, Director of Policy Planning, who was given the same title in a new position created in the White House; and Margaret Tutweiler, Baker's spokesperson who was moved to the position of White House Communications Director.

Dennis Ross, as had Clayton Yeutter, became the senior domestic policy advisor and again added another layer between Roger Porter and the president. Porter's influence in policy development continued to ebb.

The Baker team aggressively moved to develop a new approach to domestic policy, an approach that could capture the imagination and the votes of the American electorate. But Baker, who was also named campaign manager, became preoccupied with the daily problems of running the campaign. The White House returned to its reactive role, reacting to Clinton's charges of a failed domestic agenda. As he had in 1988, Bush ran a negative campaign in 1992 attacking the Democratic challengers for their liberal, tax-and-spend ways rather than touting the accomplishments of his own administration.

When the voters spoke, they turned out the foreign-policy president and brought in a new, domestic-policy president, Bill Clinton. As one columnist noted of George Bush, "he plots a campaign that will be another symbolic compact of political gestures and formalisms. It is the only sort of campaign he seems to know how to wage. Once more into the vacuum."[69]

---

[68]Andrew Rosenthal, "Baker Leaving State Department To Head White House Staff and Guide Bush's Campaign," *New York Times*, August 14, 1992, p A1.
[69]Sidney Blumenthal, "The Half President," *New Republic*, September 30, 1991, p 13.

simultaneously with little coordination: the cabinet search, the agency cluster teams, and the vetters. The result was a cabinet that shared few guiding principles and department staff that shared even fewer guiding principles.

The absence of a set of guiding principles for the department heads and their staffs again mirrored the candidate himself. The Clinton campaign was built on the concept of rebuilding the American economy, with few specifics of how or when. At the same time the campaign was promising to rebuild the economy, it was promising to cut government spending and reduce the federal deficit. Liberal Democrats were therefore comfortable that the new administration would support programs for the underprivileged and that preserved the environment, encouraged education, and protected the very young and very old. Conservative Democrats were comfortable that the new administration would cut the deficit and restore fiscal integrity to the federal budget, and the New Democrats were comfortable that a little of both would be accomplished.

The administration that emerged during the fall of 1992 was one with a wide range of personalities, each with a different view on goals and objectives. Few knew each other; few had worked together previously; few knew Clinton; and few shared a common vision. The team brought together by Bill Clinton to run the executive branch lacked a sense of commitment to either a broad goal or to Bill Clinton. This later proved to be a key problem as Clinton moved toward achieving a strong domestic agenda.

The Transition: Building a White House Staff

Clinton's determination to build a diverse cabinet was to some degree paralleled in the White House. The Clinton White House had more women and minorities than any White House in history, although it failed to achieve the level of diversity planned. His senior staff of nineteen included only two African Americans (Alexis Herman, director of public liaison) and Margaret Williams (Hillary Rodham Clinton's chief of staff), and one Hispanic (Regina Montoya, director of intergovernmental affairs).[23] The five senior staff women, these three plus domestic policy advisor Carol Rasco and scheduler Marcia Hale, provided gender balance, although not the level that was originally sought. Clinton's determination to bring women and minorities into the administration was generally easier at the deputy and special-assistant level, since most of the members were chosen from paper credentials and not personal relationships. More than one-third of the top fifty-nine jobs were given to women.

The White House senior staff, however, was pulled primarily from the campaign, as White House staffs traditionally are. This proved a stumbling

[23]Burt Solomon, "Boomers in Charge," *National Journal*, June 19, 1993, p 1457.

block in the move toward diversification, since most of Clinton's top campaign staff were white men. Clinton's efforts toward diversification were more successful at the junior staff level. Women and minorities were incorporated into every division of the White House.

Many of these junior staff were also young, averaging in their twenties, right out of college and graduate school. So many junior staff were right out of school that the White House was often referred to as "the campus."[24]

As his chief of staff, Clinton appointed his childhood friend and campaign advisor, a Little Rock energy executive, Thomas "Mack" McLarty. As his national security advisor, Clinton appointed the campaign foreign policy advisor, Mt. Holyoke College professor Anthony Lake. For his economic policy advisor, Clinton chose his campaign economic advisor, Goldman-Sachs executive Robert Rubin. All were white men. Tapped for domestic policy advisor was Bruce Reed, the campaign domestic policy coordinator. But Reed was moved to the second tier for the sake of gender diversity and a senior staff member from Arkansas, Carol Rasco, was brought in to direct domestic policy. The only other senior woman was Ricki Seidman, appointed first as deputy chief of staff and then scheduling director. In spite of lofty goals toward diversification, the inner circle remained predominantly male and all white. Only one minority, Alexis Herman, who had served as deputy director of the Democratic National Party, gained senior status in her capacity as Assistant to the President for Public Liaison. The position was not a policy-making position however, and Herman was peripheral to the inner circle.

In addition to the top policy-making positions, Clinton appointed several other white men to senior staff positions. Bernard Nussbaum became Counsel to the President, Vincent Foster, deputy counsel, and Mark Gearan, deputy chief of staff. Gearan later moved to the communications post. George Stephanopoulos, who had been the primary spokesperson for the campaign, moved to the position first of communications director in the White House and then senior policy advisor. The press secretary position went to campaign press secretary DeeDee Myers. Myers, who had senior status, was never considered a key member of the decision-making team and eventually resigned because of her lack of participation in decisions. She resigned on December 31, 1994, and was replaced by a white male, Michael McCurry, who had been the State Department's press secretary. McCurry demanded and received a seat at all senior staff meetings (Figure 7.1).

The result was a senior staff with whom Clinton was comfortable. They had toiled with him throughout the campaign and remained loyal when many had left the fold. Their loyalty was to Bill Clinton rather than to a set of ideals or to a philosophy of government. Their goal was to change the way government operates and to refocus the nation on domestic rather than international issues. They had few specific objectives or mechanisms for

[24]Michael Duffy, "The Kids Down the Hall," *Time*, March 8, 1993, p 44.

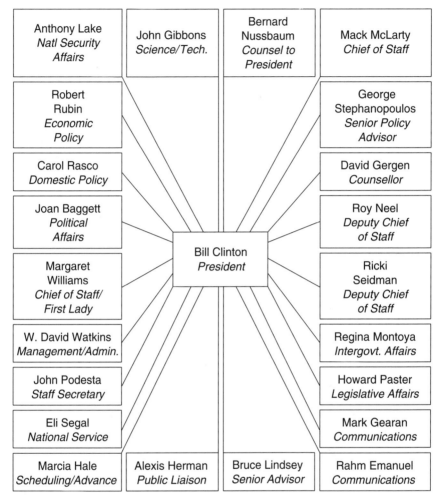

Figure 7.1   Senior White House Staff, 1993
Source: U.S. Government Manual.

moving their broad goals forward. In contrast, however, the cabinet officers had numerous specific objectives they wanted to move forward. The personnel choices that Clinton made for his White House staff and cabinet would soon lead the administration into policy chaos.

The Transition: Setting a Domestic Agenda

In an effort to establish at least economic goals for the fledgling administration, Clinton held a two-day conference in Little Rock on the economy in mid-December. Over 400 economists, business executives, technology experts, state and local government officials, and Wall Street wizards were invited by the transition staff to meet with the president-elect to discuss the economy. The conference was divided into a one-day session on "Assessment of the Domestic Economy" and a one-day session on "Assessment of the International Economy." Each session was designed to provide an economic agenda for the new administration in both domestic and international economic policy. Every national news program opened its segment with coverage of the president-elect strategically discussing economic policy with the nation's economic leaders. The economic conference succeeded in refocusing attention away from the appointments process, which had not been well-received by the general public. Although few specific goals emerged from the conference, attention was diverted from the cabinet selection process to the economy. It was a brilliant public relations move by the transition team. The economic summit had bought time but had not minimized the need for a strategy for dealing with the domestic agenda.

As the transition continued, Clinton gathered his newly appointed White House staff to prepare a list of actions that could be immediately pursued, through legislative initiative or executive order, successfully. The White House policy groups, led by Bruce Reed, identified executive orders as the most likely avenue for success, and listed such possibilities as lifting the gag rule on abortion counseling in federally funded clinics, the return of Haitian boat people without a hearing, the ban on fetal tissue testing, and converting a percentage of the government automotive fleet to natural gas.[25] Each of these executive orders would satisfy a campaign promise and would allow the administration to "hit the ground running," as they wanted to do.

One major issue that Clinton intended to address as soon as the administration took office was the banning of homosexuals in the military. Clinton had captured the gay vote by promising to aggressively seek a reversal by the military on their position concerning homosexuals. Soon after winning the election, Clinton asked Washington, D.C., lawyer John Holum to meet with top military officials to discuss how to deal with the issue. Holum, who had been active in the Clinton campaign as a foreign policy and defense advisor, had served in the State Department under Jimmy Carter and was currently a partner of Warren Christopher at O'Melveny and Myers.[26] Although Holum was a logical intermediary for Clinton, he was still considered second tier by the miliary establishment. This process succeeded in drawing the wrath of

[25]Al Kamen, "Helping a Jogger Hit the Ground Running", *Washington Post*, December 4, 1992, p A29.
[26]John D. Holum was named by Clinton as director, Arms Control and Disarmament Agency (ACDA). See Jeffrey B. Trammell and Gary P. Osifchin, The Clinton 500: *The New Team Running America 1994* (Washington, D.C.: Almanac Publishing, Inc., 1994).

the military and of senior members of Congress, who were concerned that Clinton had not met with them personally.

Clinton's decision to use Holum was another example of a transition process that had little order, little focus, and little continuity. It was a relatively simple decision by Clinton to have Holum pursue the issue, rather than a well-thought out plan for the transition. This was typical decision making during the transition, in which Clinton made decisions with little group input or discussion. Clinton orchestrated numerous parts of the transition and remained fully involved in the cabinet selection process, developing lists of names with his senior staff and reviewing the assets and liability of each candidate. Once the president-elect had been brought two names, each candidate was asked to Little Rock for an interview. Clinton took the interviews extremely seriously, and often changed his mind about the front-runner after the interview. Alice Rivlin, for example, was the front-runner for director of the Office of Management and Budget, but, for whatever reason, the interview went badly and Clinton chose Rep. Leon Panetta (D- Calif) for the job.

Clinton's submergence in the cabinet selection process, his micromanagement of the economic summit in December, and his review of sub-cabinet positions to ensure ethnic, gender, and geographic diversity dominated his time. Those designated for the White House staff were busy dealing with the agency cluster groups, the economic summit, and the executive orders. Discussions on developing a domestic agenda and structuring a White House staff to manage the domestic agenda moved to the forefront of the transition agenda as December snows began to fall.

The Transition: The Domestic Agenda

By the end of December, discussions had finally emerged within the transition team on how to most effectively structure the White House staff to manage the domestic agenda. Clinton wanted to redesign the Reagan-Bush staffing model, which had a national security staff and a domestic policy staff, with a new model that added an economic policy staff, in a plan similar to the Ford structure. This was due largely to the urging of Robert Reich, who wanted to see an "Economic Security Council" added to the White House decision-making structure.[27] Clinton agreed and supported a three-pronged approach to policy development: domestic, economic, and national security. Al Gore pursued an additional prong to policy development and successfully added environmental policy to the model. The model that was eventually approved for the White House included the National Security Council and the Office of Policy Development (OPD) as the two primary policy development units. Within the OPD, three separate divisions were created: the

[27]Bob Woodward, *The Agenda* (New York: Simon and Schuster, 1994), p 47.

Domestic Policy Council, the National Economic Council, and the Environmental Policy Council.

Two of the three staff directors within the OPD, Carol Rasco and Robert Rubin, were given the title Assistant to the President and given direct access to Clinton. Environmental policy director, Kathleen McGinty, was given the title Deputy Assistant to the President, an indication of the influence she would have in White House decision making (Figure 7.2).

The chief of staff, who traditionally oversees the policy units, chose not to oversee policy development, as Bush's chief of staff John Sununu had done. McLarty took the job with the notion that he would not review policy proposals going to the president or curtail staff from seeing the president (Figure 7.3). In an interview, McLarty said that he did not intend to be "an aggressive gatekeeper... Bill Clinton is obviously a very engaged person. He is going to be deciding what gets to his desk."[28] McLarty supported Clinton's concept of a spokes-of-the-wheel operating system, which encouraged an open door to the Oval Office by senior staff. McLarty viewed his role primarily as the manager of the day-to-day operations of the White House and "to organize the workers in a professional, timely, efficient manner."[29]

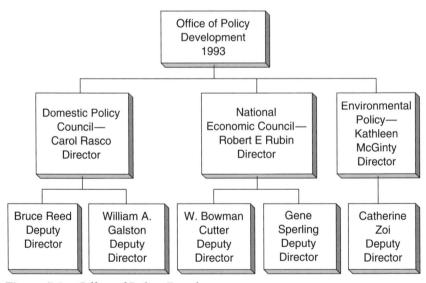

Figure 7.2   Office of Policy Development
Source: Federal Staff Directory, Ltd.

[28]Michael Kelly, "Clinton's Chief of Staff Ponders Undefined Post," *New York Times,* December 14, 1992, p B6.
[29]Op. cit.

McLarty's decision not to oversee policy issues allowed senior White House staff to determine their own levels of power. Since Clinton had determined economic affairs to be the cornerstone of the administration, Robert Rubin, Assistant to the President for Economic Affairs and director of the National Economic Council, immediately moved to develop an economic strategy. Carol Rasco, Assistant to the President for Domestic Policy and director of the Domestic Policy Council, immediately moved to develop a domestic strategy. Kathleen McGinty, director of the Office of Environmental Policy, chose to work closely with the Environmental Protection Agency and the Interior Department and not to move the White House into the forefront of environmental decision making.

The problems that the Clinton administration encountered as they pursued a domestic agenda began when the White House separated economic policy from domestic policy and divided both the energy and the resources of the White House staff. Neither the campaign staff nor the transition staff identified those issues and agenda items on which the White House would focus. Had Clinton prepared a clearly focused, well-articulated plan for dealing with the economy or the domestic agenda prior to the election, or prepared such a plan during the transition, the inherent conflicts between the two policy units would have been minimized. But no such plan was prepared, and the two units were faced with preparing their own agendas, integrating those agendas where possible, and competing for limited financial support for those agendas. The result was a haphazard approach to domestic policy making that often was consumed by firefighting activities rather than policy development.

The Domestic Policy Council:
Developing an Organizational Structure

At the core of the domestic policy-making apparatus in the White House was the Domestic Policy Council under the direction of Carol Rasco (Figure 7.4). Rasco had worked with Clinton in a variety of capacities in Little Rock since 1976. She first was appointed by Clinton to the Arkansas Mental Retardation and Developmental Disabilities Board and then as the governor's liaison for health and human services. She eventually moved into the position as co-chief of staff. During Clinton's tenure as vice chairman and chairman of the National Governor's Association in 1989 and 1990, Rasco was the point person on welfare reform. She had a strong working relationship with Clinton and with members of the campaign team.

Although Al Gore had successfully lobbied Clinton to elevate environmental policy to the level of White House decision making and had successfully moved a member of his staff, Katie McGinty, into the position, Clinton did not give the environmental unit the same weight that either domestic or

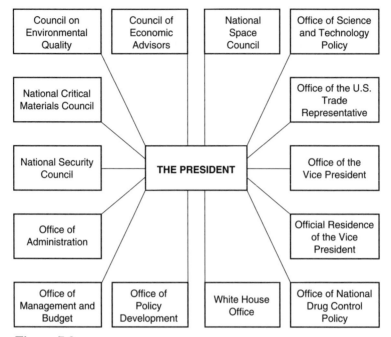

Figure 7.3
Source: U.S. Government Manual

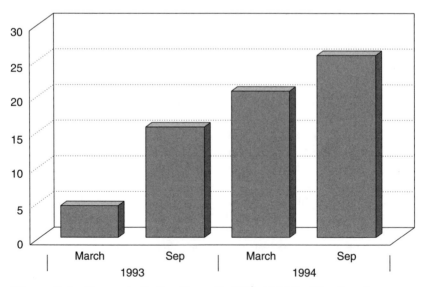

Figure 7.4   Domestic Policy Council, 1993–1994 Staffing Levels
Source: Federal Staff Directory, Ltd.

economic policy were given. While Rasco and Rubin were accorded senior staff status with the title "Assistant to the President," McGinty was given the title "Deputy Assistant to the President." Her age, 29, and her experience on Gore's staff mitigated her power within the White House. McGinty quickly realized that Rasco and Rubin would dominate the policy process with the president, and therefore skillfully turned her attentions to working through the vice president and his nominee at the Environmental Protection Agency, Carol Browner. At 29, McGinty was the youngest senior staff member, although numerous staff in their twenties and thirties roamed the corridors of the White House, leading some to refer to the White House staff as "Clinton's Brady Kids."[30]

Rasco's major competition for managing the domestic agenda was Robert Rubin, director of the National Economic Council. Rubin, who had served as a major fundraiser for Clinton during the election, had not worked with Rasco and barely knew her. They had not worked together during the campaign nor during the transition, leading to a difficult situation once they both took their offices in the west wing. Although their tasks were to develop a domestic agenda for the administration, they approached their tasks separately and with little coordination. Even though their staffs were housed on the same hall in the Old Executive Office Building, they each had their own organizations and their own agendas. In the absence of a chief of staff to coordinate issues, Rasco and Rubin were each given total control over how they approached their policy-making responsibilities.

Domestic Policy Making: Creating an Organization

The approach taken by Rasco was one that viewed policy development as integrally related and conceptually crosscutting. As Jeff Faux, president of the Economic Policy Institute noted, Clinton's vision for policy development involved "the connections between transportation and energy and creating jobs and business development in cities."[31] That vision of overlapping issues dominated the way the White House was organized for domestic policy development. The White House domestic policy apparatus created a general policy goal and then pulled together working groups of department senior staff to work out the details.

The working groups were technically part of the cabinet council known as the Domestic Policy Council, composed of the entire cabinet except for Defense and State, and a host of White House senior staff. The Domestic Policy Council was created by executive order to create a cabinet-based policy

[30]Matthew Cooper, "Clinton's Brady Kids," *U.S. News and World Report*, January 18, 1993, p 32–33.
[31]Burt Solomon, "A One-Man Band," *National Journal*, April 24, 1993, p 971.

mechanism for coordinating and developing domestic policy.[32] Premised on the Domestic Council created by Richard Nixon in 1970, Clinton's Domestic Policy Council was a formal mechanism for assembling the domestic cabinet to manage domestic policy. However, in contrast to Nixon's 1970 Domestic Council executive order that limited participation to cabinet officers, the 1993 Domestic Policy Council included White House staff as members.

The executive order created a Domestic Policy Council consisting of the president, the vice president, the attorney general, the secretaries of Agriculture, Commerce, Education, Health and Human Services, Housing and Urban Development, Interior, Labor, Transportation, Treasury, Veterans Affairs, and the administrator of the Environmental Protection Agency, the director of the Office of Management and Budget, the Assistant to the President for Domestic Policy, the Assistant to the President for Economic Policy, the Assistant to the President and the Director of the Office of National Service, the Senior Advisor to the President for Policy Development, the director of National Drug Control Policy, and the national AIDS policy coordinator. Every member of the cabinet except Defense and State was included in the council.

Through the executive order, the Domestic Policy Council was given broad authority to manage the administration's domestic agenda but focused their efforts on coordination. The executive order provided for the Domestic Policy Council to

1. coordinate the domestic policy making process,
2. coordinate domestic policy advice to the President,
3. ensure that domestic policy decisions and programs are consistent with the President's stated goals and to ensure that those goals are being effectively pursued, and
4. monitor implementation of the President's domestic policy agenda.[33]

The White House domestic policy staff, who continued to play the dominant role in policy development and agenda setting, viewed the process as an opportunity "to reduce the inherent tension between those who develop and those who execute policy," as Carol Rasco noted.[34] But for Rasco and her staff, the Domestic Policy Council was a tool of policy coordination rather than a tool of policy development or management. The Domestic Policy Council staff saw the executive order as providing a structural mechanism to coordinate existing policy. Creating new policy initiatives was secondary to the focus of the domestic policy staff. They did not view themselves as the center of administration agenda setting or policy making.

[32]Executive Order #12895, August 17, 1993.
[33]Executive Order #12895.
[34]Interview with Carol Rasco.

Rasco did move, however, to gain control over some aspects of the policy process. The Domestic Policy Council was convened in the White House to ensure that cabinet members understood that the White House managed domestic policy. Full Domestic Policy Council meetings were held every other Monday from 5:30 P.M. to 6:30 P.M. in the Roosevelt Room. Their purpose was to share information on major issues and discuss presidential priorities. Neither the president nor the vice president attended, leaving Rasco to chair the meetings.

The full Domestic Policy Council operated only to ensure that cabinet officers considered themselves full partners in the policy process. The constant interaction of cabinet officers and White House staff was designed to serve one purpose: to ensure that cabinet officers considered themselves members of the president's staff and not member's of the department staff. Rasco continually tried to reinforce to the cabinet that they were a key part of the president's team and the decision-making process.

The actual work of policy making was done outside of the formal Domestic Policy Council in what was referred to as "the working groups." Working groups were ad hoc groups, put together by Rasco, that focused on specific issues. A working group was created to deal with an issue and was disbanded once the issue was satisfactorily addressed. According to Bruce Reed, Deputy Assistant to the President for Domestic Policy, "the working groups were formed with a specific goal in mind and to come up with legislation to accomplish that goal. Once that goal is reached and the legislation is passed, the working group will cease to exist."[35]

Working groups were generally co-chaired by members of the White House staff and senior departmental staff. For example, the working group on welfare reform had thirty-three members from various agencies and had three co-chairs. Those co-chairs were Bruce Reed and two assistant secretaries from Health and Human Services. The working groups prepared recommendations that were presented to the larger Domestic Policy Council for their review. Once the recommendations were approved by the DPC, Rasco met with the president. Working groups generally developed several options that were given to the president for his decision. Once the president made a decision on an option, the White House staff sent the proposal back to the working group for a revised product.

The process created by Rasco tried to center policy initiation in the White House, with Rasco's office determining the policy issues that the working groups would focus on, creating the membership of the working groups, and chairing the meetings. The departments were secondary players in the policy process as the organizational structure was laid out. The structure satisfied Clinton's determination to build teams in his administration,

[35]Interview with Bruce Reed.

since his view of organizational behavior was premised on the concept of teamwork. For Clinton, teamwork was essential to ensuring a sense of loyalty to administration goals and minimizing attempts by departments to dominate issues on behalf of their clientele.[36] The teamwork concept reduced interdepartmental conflict and the age-old problem of turf wars. As Bruce Reed described the process, teamwork and the working groups contributed to a "blurring" of departmental lines while policy issues were being hashed out.[37]

Cracks in the Organization

While Carol Rasco and her staff tried to craft a structure for policy development that minimized departmental warfare and kept the White House staff in control of setting the agenda, cracks in the structure began to appear from the outset of the administration.

The first problem that emerged was Clinton's determination to oversee the domestic policy agenda. Clinton, after two days on the job with a daily national security briefing, wanted similar daily briefings from Rasco and Rubin. Each morning Rasco and Rubin met separately with Clinton, for 15–20 minutes, to discuss key issues moving through their councils. Clinton wanted to personally review all of the recommendations emerging from the policy working groups and to have regular briefings on the activities of the Domestic Policy Council and the National Economic Council staffs. Once decisions were made by the working groups, Clinton called key members of the group and his own staff together to discuss the options. Clinton relished sitting in the Roosevelt Room with the working groups and hearing the various options available. He often rejected all of the options and asked for further review and another meeting. According to Robert Rubin, Clinton "likes to have policy issues go by him. He likes to see options."[38] This process began to lengthen the time frame, as the working groups met repeatedly to frame the initial policy options and then continued to meet to narrow the options to satisfy the president.

As a result, during the first year of the administration, few major policy initiatives emerged. Health care reform, welfare reform, and urban revitalization, all central to the campaign's platform for the domestic agenda, were tied in knots by the wide-ranging concept of working groups. The process for policy development had in effect stifled decision making and encouraged lengthy policy discussions with numerous players. Frustrated by the constant feet dragging by the departments, the White House tried to ensure that the public saw an activist president. They began to zero in on issues that did not require departmental involvement or that were not perceived as interdepartmental.

[36]Shirley Anne Warshaw, *Powersharing: White House-Cabinet Relations in the Modern Presidency* (Albany, New York: SUNY Press, 1996).
[37]Burt Solomon, "A One-Man Band," *National Journal*, April 24, 1993, p 971.
[38]Op cit.

The Domestic Agenda of 1993

As the White House domestic policy staff moved to focus on issues that could be easily resolved and provide the president the accomplishments that he needed early in the term, they turned to the list of priorities that Clinton laid out at the outset of the administration. In a retreat held for cabinet and senior White House staff at Camp David during the weekend of January 30–31, 1993, Clinton listed five priorities for the administration:

- a stimulus program to reinvigorate the job base;
- an economic program that reduced the deficit and shifted priorities from consumption to investment;
- a political reform bill, including reform of campaign financing and new restrictions on lobbying;
- comprehensive reform of health care; and
- a national service bill.[39]

The absence of any easily attainable domestic programs on the list reinforced the problems that the White House staff faced in gaining control of the domestic agenda. The two top issues on the list were being managed by Rubin's National Economic Council; the political reform bill was managed by the Congressional liaison staff; health care reform, although technically part of the Domestic Policy Council purview, was tightly held by Ira Magaziner and Hillary Clinton. Similarly, the national service bill was controlled by Eli Segal and his staff in the White House. That left no major issue for the Domestic Policy Council staff to tackle and no clear agenda from which to frame its own issues.

In February, the Domestic Policy Council staff was hit with another setback. On February 9, 1993, Clinton announced that 350 positions would be trimmed from the White House staff.[40] This was part of a larger effort to show that the administration was serious about curbing the federal bureaucracy. The cuts included not only White House staff but all departments. Cabinet departments and agencies were ordered to cut 100,000 jobs from the federal workforce of 2.1 million by the end of 1995 and to trim administrative costs by an average of 3% per year. Such administrative cost savings were intended to save 14% over the next four years for a total saving of $9 billion.

The staffing losses that the general White House staff were faced with, however, did not include the National Economic Council. In mid-March,

[39]Elizabeth Drew, *On the Edge: The Clinton Presidency* (New York: Simon and Schuster, 1995), p 52.
[40]Most of the reductions to the White House staff were in the National Drug Control Policy Office, which went from 146 to 25 positions. In addition, 117 detailees to the White House were returned to the departments.

W. Bowman Cutter, deputy director of the NEC, went before the House Appropriations Subcommittee on Treasury, Postal Service and General Government and requested a 36% increase, or $5.1 million, in its budget.[41] Cutter, who said the overall Office of Policy Development staff was being reduced as Clinton had mandated throughout the White House, said the National Economic Council staff was slightly increasing.

The National Economic Council Dominates Policy Making

The sudden emergence of the National Economic Council rather than the Domestic Policy Council as the key player within the Office of Policy Development was due to Clinton's decision to focus on economic rather than domestic issues (Figure 7.5). Immediately after the inauguration, Clinton announced to his staff that the economic plan that he would present to Congress would be the center of attention at the White House. He ordered all senior staff, including both the economic and domestic policy teams, to work on the plan, "day and night and weekends if necessary."[42] The group met in the Roosevelt Room, constantly reviewing options put on the table by both the cabinet and White House staff.

A wide assortment of proposals moved back and forth among the group. Magaziner wanted price controls on health care. Clinton rejected the idea. Panetta urged freezing Social Security cost of living adjustments (COLAs), Congressional opposition ended the discussion. Gene Sperling, deputy director of the National Economic Council, urged Clinton to fulfill his campaign promise of "rewarding work" through an expanded earned income tax credit. Clinton agreed. The energy tax concept again emerged and became a key point in the economic plan. Higher taxes on the upper income brackets became another accepted point in the plan. Finally, Mrs. Clinton prevailed in ensuring that, whatever economic package moved forward, health care reform was to be included.

After February 7, 1993, when Clinton spoke to the nation from the Oval Office to explain his economic proposals, the White House focused its energies on moving the economic stimulus plan, as it became known, through Congress. Howard Paster and his Congressional liaison team joined the National Economic Council as the quarterbacks of the White House team. In June, 1993, in an effort to break the logjam with Congress and build public support for the plan, Clinton brought *U.S. News and World Report* managing editor David Gergen onto the White House staff. Gergen had been a senior member of the Nixon and Reagan staffs, managing the communica-

---

[41]Timothy Burger, "White House Agencies Ask Hefty Budget Hikes," *Roll Call*, March 22, 1993, p 15.
[42]Bob Woodward, *The Agenda*, p 121.

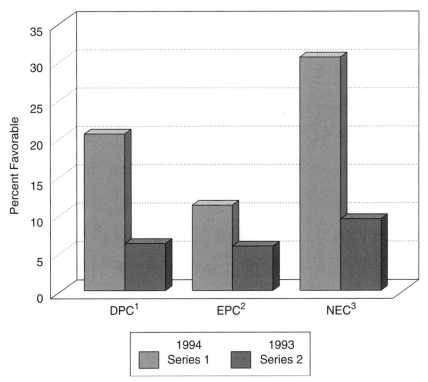

Figure 7.5   Office of Policy Development, 1993–1994 Staffing Levels
[1]DPC, Domestic Policy Council
[2]EPC, Environmental Policy Council
[3]NEC, National Educational Council
Source: Federal Staff Directory, Ltd.

tions efforts and overall public relations. Gergen's Republican ties to Congress and his experience in moving presidential policies through the media provided a new depth to the White House staff.

As the president continued to focus on economic issues and his stimulus program in 1993, the domestic agenda was pushed to the backburner of the decision process. Clinton was being attacked by both Democrats and Republicans for his economic plan. Typical of the statements that were emerging in editorials was, "Clinton is the two-headed monster that is raising our taxes, cutting our defenses, and still adding the equivalent of eight and a half years of Reagan deficits to the economy in only four years."[43] Although this

[43]Paul Craig Roberts, "Ten Steps Backward," *National Review*, March 29, 1993, p 52.

appeared in the conservative *National Review*, its general theme, although less harsh, was repeated in editorials across the country. Rasco's structure for policy making had focused on the working groups, which were charged with forging policy proposals. But their charge was vague and their time frame undefined. In contrast, Treasury Secretary Lloyd Bentsen, his deputy Robert Altman, and Robert Rubin and his staff had a mandate from the president and quickly moved to develop specific proposals.

Eli Segal, who had a similarly specific charge from the president, moved rapidly toward building Congressional support for a National Service Corporation. In late January, 1993, only days after taking office, Segal was meeting with members of Congress on the national service plan.[44]

Watching the unfolding of the power structure in the White House was Robert Reich, Labor Secretary. Reich, who had sought the Treasury Secretary job but was turned down by Clinton because of his lack of support from Wall Street, refused to be relegated to the secondary Domestic Policy Council. Reich saw the Domestic Policy Council as a minor player in policy making and sought to focus his efforts on economic policy making, which had the president's attention. Reich continually tried to influence White House proposals by sending Clinton notes. He successfully maneuvered a section in the economic stimulus plan to include federal funding for more technological and highly skilled training. His plan called for a youth apprenticeship program for the 40 percent of high school graduates that don't go to college.[45] He similarly successfully urged that more funds be allocated to pay for rebuilding the nation's infrastructure, tied to a jobs plan.

By the summer of 1993, six months after taking office, the Domestic Policy Council staff had few major accomplishments. The economic stimulus plan had dominated Clinton's energies and its deficit-cutting themes had delayed any significant domestic initiatives. Health care reform, managed outside Rasco and her staff, dominated the domestic agenda. The only significant area for which the Domestic Policy Council staff had successfully produced a major proposal was welfare reform, aimed at using state welfare-to-work programs as a model.[46] This program, however, was immediately targeted by Senator Daniel Patrick Moynihan (D-NY), whose Education and Labor Committee would control the debate in the Senate. Moynihan, rather than being opposed to the program, chafed at being left out of the policy discussions with Rasco.

The public was becoming disenchanted with the president who had campaigned on change and a strong domestic agenda (Figure 7.6). Polls showed Clinton had the lowest approval rating since Gerald Ford's pardon of Richard Nixon.

---

[44]"National Service Plan," *Congressional Quarterly*, January 30, 1993, p 218.
[45]Rochelle L. Stanfield, "Ugly Duckling," *National Journal*, February 6, 1993, p 335.
[46]"Use State Welfare-to-Work Programs As Model," *Congressional Quarterly*, June 5, 1993.

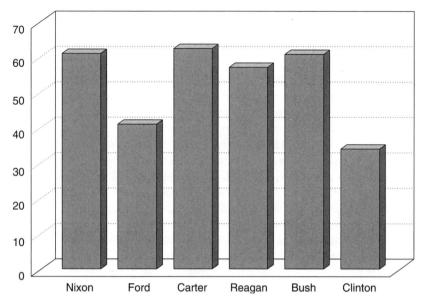

Figure 7.6   Clinton's Approval Rating, Spring 1993
Source: The Gallup Organization

Refocusing the Agenda

As the legislative fights heated up over the economic stimulus package and health care reform, foreign policy issues began moving to the forefront of Clinton's daily agenda. Somalia and Bosnia, crises inherited from the Bush administration, were constantly requiring decisions as new policies had to be crafted that reflected the new administration's views. Decisions on aid to Russia, human rights in China, Mexican illegal immigrants, the North American Free Trade Agreement (NAFTA), the Middle East peace accords, the future of the NATO alliance, and a host of other issues began to require more of the president's time.

By the fall of 1993, after nine months in office, the White House refocused itself. Having successfully moved the economic stimulus program through Congress, Clinton wanted to target his energies on the next set of priorities, which he listed as

- government efficiency
- health care
- trade
- crime
- welfare reform.[47]

[47]"Clinton Controls Fall Agenda, Although Not Its Results," *Congressional Quarterly,* September 4, 1993, p 2296.

The issue of government efficiency was part of Al Gore's core responsibility of preparing a review of government operations that would dramatically cut costs. Gore's "reinventing government" program was well underway by September and needed no help from the Domestic Policy Council. In fact, it was clear that Gore did not want any help from Rasco or any other White House staff unit and had built his own staff to over 200 to prepare the study.

Health care was safely tucked away with Mrs. Clinton and Ira Magaziner, and trade issues were controlled by Mickey Kantor, the trade representative. That left crime and welfare reform to the Domestic Policy Council staff. The crime bill, which was a logical area for the Domestic Policy Council to focus, had heated up in August, 1993. But the Congressional liaison office gained control of that. Welfare reform was again moved to the forefront of the Domestic Policy Council staff's activities, but Moynihan had made it quite clear that he would play the lead role in initiating policy goals. Rather than jeopardize Moynihan's support for other administration bills in Congress, such as the crime bill, Rasco pulled her staff back.

As the list of major policy issues was taken over by other White House units, Rasco continued to focus on long-term planning issues and to manage the ad hoc working groups. She built closer relations with the departments and supported their policy development efforts. The move away from the National Economic Council and other White House units by the Domestic Policy Council staff was predictable. Rather than working as a "team," as Clinton had first proposed, the White House staff began moving into its own territories as more and more issues arose. The Counsel's office had its plate full with questions on support for Rep. Dan Rostenkowski (D-Ill), under investigation by the Justice Department for mishandling official funds; with Whitewater; and a host of appointments to be filled by the president. The National Economic Council was focusing on NAFTA and reducing the deficit. In mid-September Clinton and Gore went public with the reinventing government plan and gave a series of speeches around the country on its behalf. The legislation for National Service was being debated in the Senate. Health care dominated nearly every discussion in the White House. The Domestic Policy Council staff had few policies to manage and fewer policies to include in planning proposals.

As the departments watched Rasco move out of the White House powergrid, they began to promote their own programs. Donna Shalala, secretary of Health and Human Services, aggressively pursued funding for the preschool program "Headstart" and federally supported immunizations for underprivileged children. The National Aeronautics and Space Agency (NASA) sought continued funding for the Freedom space station. The Justice Department announced plans for an activist civil rights division. Energy Secretary Hazel O'Leary called for more funding for nuclear reactors. The National Institutes of Health, a division of HHS, sought increased AIDS

dency to reflect the themes of the New Democrats again, themes that had often been lost in the first two years of the administration. Bruce Reed and Bill Galston, Rasco's two chief deputies who had worked with the departments to craft policy proposals, were moved to the forefront of policy work. Reed and Galston had been leading members of the New Democratic movement, Reed as a staffer at the DLC and Galston at the University of Maryland. Panetta pulled Reed and Galston to manage the health care proposals in Congress, a job previously held by Harold Ickes. Ickes, often viewed as a liberal Democrat, was pulled off health care as a signal that the White House was refocusing its priorities. Clinton also began to add more New Democrats to the White House staff. When scheduler Ricki Seidman resigned, she was replaced by William Wendenhall Webster IV, who had been active with the DLC in South Carolina.

In a meeting with Democratic governors at the White House on November 30, 1994, a consensus emerged that the president should limit his economic and domestic agenda and establish a clearly centrist position.[55] Panetta sought to not only move the president toward a centrist policy position, but to begin to compromise with the new Republican leadership and build new programs acceptable to the new Congress. Panetta established the no-nonsense position of compromise, saying, "There's no alternative but to reach out to the Republican leadership. If there's total gridlock and partisanship, then both sides are hurt."[56] Panetta also ordered the White House staff to stop calling the Republicans names, such as the phrase "sick guy," which George Stephanopoulos used to describe the newly elected Speaker of the House, Newt Gingrich.

Rasco's Domestic Policy Council had become invisible throughout the summer and fall of 1994. When Panetta met with the departments to discuss new policy strategies for the remainder of the administration, Rasco was not included.[57] As Clinton moved toward reconciliation with the new Congress, his primary advisors were Panetta, Stephanopoulos, and Rubin. Rasco was not at the center of decision making. Clinton's strategy for setting the national agenda was one of emphasizing common ground with the Republicans, of focusing on those items in the "Contract with America" that he supported. Rather than including Rasco in designing a new domestic strategy that could be adapted to Republican goals, he simply kept her out of the decision-making loop.

As a result, the working groups continued to focus on the projects that they had begun earlier in the administration. When Panetta met with the

[55]Ann Devroy, "President Struggling to Stake out Strategy and Take the Offensive," *Washington Post*, November 30, 1994, p A4.
[56]Susan Garland, "Trying to Tame A Wild Elephant," *Business Week*, November 28, 1994, p 50.
[57]Ann Devroy, "President Struggling to Stake Out Strategy and Take the Offensive," *Washington Post*, November 30, 1994, p A4.

chiefs of staff of each agency after the election, he did not refocus their agenda or provide new goals and objectives.[58] They left the meeting confused and under the impression they should continue to focus on the policy proposals initiated in the working groups.

As the new year began in 1995, Clinton continued to distance himself from Rasco and the Domestic Policy Council (Figure 7.8). Although Rasco had been given no direct orders to revamp the domestic policy process, Clin-

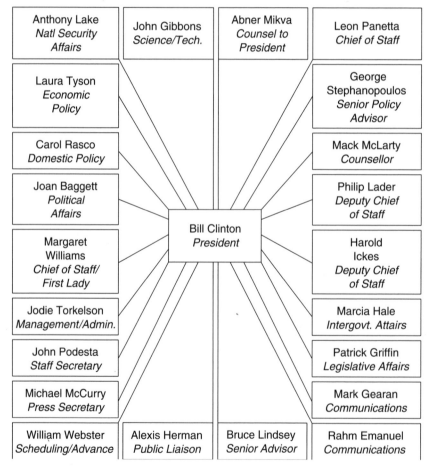

Figure 7.8
Senior White House Staff, 1995

[58]Op cit.

ton began to work around her and her staff. The major policy announcement on restructuring the way agencies were run came from Gore's office rather than Rasco's office. Gore announced that the administration planned to fold sixty programs at the Department of Housing and Urban Development into three block grant programs for public housing, rent assistance, and community development. This, according to Gore, would save the government $13 billion over five years.[59] When Clinton wanted advice on the cost of college, he moved outside of the White House and met with twenty-five college presidents.

The Evaporation of the Domestic Agenda

By the midpoint of the administration, Clinton had aggressively moved on a jobs program, an economic stimulus program, and a national service program. All had been targeted in the campaign as priority agenda items and had been successfully accomplished. But the agenda items from the campaign that dealt with environmental issues, educational issues, children, families, welfare reform, and others had been dismally addressed.

Perhaps one explanation for this failure to secure a strong domestic agenda was that the president himself had no plan of what to address first. Although he strongly believed that government should ensure a standard of acceptable living for all Americans, he established a building-block plan for creating that standard with health care at the base. Unfortunately, the public did not agree that health care as described by the White House should be the base of a new standard. The "middle class bill of rights," promoted by Clinton in his 1995 State of the Union address, continued to lay out basic rights of every citizen, but failed to identify the key components of those rights.

Even after the disastrous November, 1994, the White House continued to operate in an almost free-for-all atmosphere. Rasco and her staff remained intact and, almost as if nothing had happened, continued to operate the working groups with the departments on domestic policy options. The options were essentially the same as those begun two years earlier. But the domestic agenda has become secondary to Clinton's economic agenda and to the efforts to cut government and reduce the deficit. Rasco's Domestic Policy Council had become a nonentity and moved away from any leadership role in policy development.

Institutionalization and the Clinton White House

The failure of the domestic policy office under Carol Rasco to articulate a set of clear policy goals and to move those goals into the forefront of the presi-

---

[59]Sonya Ross, "Clinton Proposal for HUD Greeted Unenthusiastically," *Harrisburg Patriot News,* January 25, 1995, p A4.

dent's agenda is directly related to the structure established for domestic policy making at the outset of the administration. It is not an issue of institutionalization. Domestic policy is an institutionalized process in the White House because domestic policy has become institutionalized as an integral part of presidential control over the executive branch. The process for managing domestic policy from the White House has continued under Clinton, although to a lesser degree than in other administrations.

Problems with the domestic policy apparatus are tied to a number of problems in the way domestic policy management was designed. Perhaps the most glaring problem stemmed from the campaign itself, which failed to identify a series of clear domestic policy goals. The theme of the campaign was "change" and a refocus on "domestic policy." But few specific proposals were put on the table during the campaign. That left the domestic policy office to create a set of policies. Rasco had two choices at that point: to work with the departments to frame the policies or to frame the policies in the White House and use the departments to frame implementation strategies. She chose the former. This meshed with Clinton's goal to use teams in the administration, which, he believed, ensured that the final product had broad-based support. The overarching strategy was to include as many people in the policy process as reasonable. Rasco's decision to create policy councils with the departments to deliberate policy slowed the policy process and produced wide-ranging options from which Clinton had to choose. Unlike Reagan, for example, who wanted short, concise overviews of policy options with a staff recommendation for the preferred option, Clinton wanted lengthy overviews from both department staff and White House staff on policy options. Rasco's staff did not attempt to limit departmental proposals to fit within political or fiscal parameters. Clinton, and to some degree Stephanopoulos and Gergen, were charged with providing political input into the decision process.

The options presented to the president by the departments were complicated by little consistency in the cabinet's policy orientation. With a diverse group of liberals, moderates, centrists, and conservatives in the cabinet, policy proposals brought to the president were often widely divergent. Had the transition team sought to bring greater consistency to the ideological base of the cabinet, less-divergent options would have arisen from the policy councils.

The combination of Clinton's free-flowing style of seeking numerous opinions on issues, a politically diverse cabinet, and the failure of the domestic policy office to establish narrow objectives for policy development led to a domestic policy process that was slow, cumbersome, and with few specific policy objectives. Clinton's campaign pledge to provide change was too broad for a diverse cabinet to come to grips with.

In contrast to the domestic policy operation, the economic policy operation moved smoothly, developing policy proposals and moving them through

Since the role of the domestic policy office is inherently different from the other institutionalized staff units, a high level of politicization is expected. The role of the domestic policy staff is to ensure that the executive departments understand presidential policy objectives and that departmental policies are formulated within presidential objectives. Without guidance from the White House, domestic policy would be interpreted by each of the cabinet agencies in a different manner, leading to administration-wide chaos.

Policy management and coordination are the prime roles for the domestic policy staff. The degree to which White House staff manage policy varies, even under activist presidents. Carter's domestic agenda focused less on creating or refocusing departmental policy agendas than on developing a more efficient bureaucracy and streamlined service delivery system. In contrast, Nixon's domestic agenda focused on the programmatic goals rather than the delivery process. Although the agendas varied, both Carter and Nixon had a definite domestic policy strategy that was overseen by a large White House staff unit.

Policy expertise, academic credentials, and beltway "savvy" are always critical factors in successful management in Washington. As a result, White House domestic policy offices are always populated with such staff. But the top staff and many of the other staff members are personal and political associates of the president. Their task is to ensure that those commitments made during the campaign involving domestic policy are prioritized within current political and fiscal constraints. Once a list of priority policies has been developed, the task of the domestic policy office is to ensure that all senior appointees within the departments are cognizant of those priorities and that they adjust departmental policy as necessary.

In summary, the role of the domestic policy office is to narrow the broad policy goals established during the campaign, to familiarize cabinet officers and their staffs with those goals, and to ensure that departments remain committed to implementing those goals. Goals may change throughout the course of a four-year term and be adjusted as circumstances demand. The role of the White House domestic policy staff is to ensure that, once clear objectives have been established, departmental staff understand and support those objectives and departmental policies do not overlap or duplicate functions. Policy management is the underlying role of the domestic policy staff, a role that requires more political acumen than policy experience.

The successful domestic policy advisors have been those with long personal relationships with their presidents. Daniel Patrick Moynihan, although a brilliant academician, lacked a deep understanding of Richard Nixon's domestic objectives. Similarly James Cannon, although a sterling magazine editor, lacked a deep understanding of Gerald Ford's domestic objectives. Neither Moynihan nor Cannon had any personal or professional relationship with the president before becoming domestic policy advisors. On the other side of the coin are Stuart Eizenstat and Martin Anderson. Both had worked on the campaigns, had served as domestic policy advisors on the campaigns, and were personally close to the presidents.

The success of the domestic policy office has thus far been characterized as requiring a proactive domestic policy agenda established during the campaign and a domestic policy senior staff personally committed to and knowledgeable about presidential objectives. The caveat in this model for a successful domestic policy office is the intangible component of personality. The director of the domestic policy office must be someone who forges the often wide-ranging objectives of the domestic agenda into narrow, achievable objectives.

Carol Rasco in the Clinton domestic policy office has been unsuccessful at narrowing the broad goals of the 1992 presidential campaign. Rather than allowing the White House to focus the domestic policy objectives, she created teams of departmental and White House staff to formulate policy goals. As a result, the administration failed to narrow the policy objectives within the parameters of budgetary and political constraints. Her failure was her lack of understanding of the role of the White House domestic policy office, which is to narrow the policy objectives and ensure that the departments understand and support those objectives.

Domestic Policy within the White House Organization

The structure of the White House staff has often been characterized within the literature as either a spokes-of-the-wheel structure or a hierarchial structure. Conventional wisdom described Republican presidents as tending to use the hierarchial structure and Democratic presidents as tending to use the spokes-of-the-wheel structure.

Perhaps a more accurate reading of organizational behavior should be the degree of White House management of the executive branch. In fact, every president since Richard Nixon has moved to a strong chief of staff regardless of party. Although neither Republican Gerald Ford nor Democrat Jimmy Carter entered office with a chief of staff, both added the position to control the proliferation of paper and people vying for presidential attention. The role of chief of staff has become essential as the federal government has continued to increase its mandated responsibilities and thus the oversight role of the White House has further burgeoned.

As a consequence of the inevitability of the office of chief of staff in the modern presidency, the domestic policy advisor will generally not report directly to the president. Rather, domestic policy advisors have reported to the president through the chief of staff. The only exception was Stuart Eizenstat, who briefly had direct access to Carter before Hamilton Jordan

Office of Drug Abuse Policy, 95*n*.
Office of Executive Management (OEM),
   35–36, 50
Office of Management and Budget (OMB),
   9, 11
   Bush, 163, 171
   Carter, 93–94, 102, 96*n*.
   Clinton, 189
   Ford, 63, 75
   Nixon, 38, 42
   Reagan, 127, 130, 132, 136
Office of Policy Development (OPD), 11,
   122–137, 142, 144
Office of Policy Information, 129, 130
Office of Telecommunications Policy, 95*n*.
O'Leary, Hazel, 202
O'Leary, James J., 23
O'Neill, Thomas P. "Tip", 94

Panetta, Leon
   Clinton: chief of staff, 205, 206, 207;
      and Office of Management and Budget,
      189, 198
   Nixon: HEW, 48
Paster, Howard, 187, 198
Pena, Federico, 183
Pentagon Papers, 54
Perot, Ross, 180
Pierce, Samuel, 120
Pierre Hotel, 19, 23
Pifer, Alan, 23
Pinkerton, James, 146, 165*n*.
   Office of Policy Planning, 165–167, 169
   the 100-day plan, 154
   transition, 151–154
Podesta, John, 187, 204, 206
Poindexter, John, 142*n*.
Policy Coordinating Group, 175–176
Porter, Roger, 59–60
   Bush: Asst. to the President for Economic
      and Domestic Policy, 159, 160, 163–171,
      163*n*., 164*n*.; transition, 155; Clean Air
      Act, 168, 170–171
   Reagan: Office of Policy Development,
      129, 130, 131, 132, 134, 137
Postal Revenue and Federal Salary Act of
   1967, 24*n*.
Powell, Jody, 85–86, 86*n*.
President's Advisory Committee on
   Government Organization (PACGO),
   35–36, 35*n*.

President's Advisory Council on Executive
   Organization (PACEO), 35, 38, 40*n*.
President's Committee on Government
   Organization (PACGO), 7, 9
Presidential Transition Act of 1963, 118*n*.
Price, John, 29

Quayle, J. Danforth, 145, 159, 173
Quern, Arthur, 76

Rasco, Carol
   domestic policy advisor, 185–186, 204, 206
   Domestic Policy Council, 190–200, 202,
      207–210
   working groups, 195–196
Reagan, Nancy, 113, 113*n*.
Reagan, Ronald, 2–3
   Cabinet Affairs Office, 136
   cabinet councils, 125–127, 130, 131, 132,
      135, 143
   Cabinet Government, 129
   campaign of 1976, 112
   domestic policy council, 135, 137
   economic policy council, 135
   election of 1976, 112
   election of 1980, 111–117
   election of 1984, 133
   General Electric, 114
   Goldwater, Barry, 111
   Governor of California, 111–112
   Iran-Contra, 140–142
   Office of Cabinet Administration, 127
   Office of Policy Development (OPD),
      122–137, 142
   Reagan Revolution, 111, 114–117, 121,
      126, 134–135, 138–139
   second term, 133–143
   transition of 1980, 117–122
Reagan-Bush Planning Task Force, 119
Reed, Bruce, 186, 188, 190, 195–196, 207
Regan, Donald
   chief of staff, 133–138, 140–141
   Iran-Contra, 140–141
   resignation, 141
   Treasury, 119, 128–129
Reich, Robert, 183, 189, 200
Reilly, William K., 161, 169
Reorganization Act of 1939, 81, 94
Republican Party
   and Ford, 69, 81
   and Nixon, 20

Reykjavik Summit, 140
Richardson, Elliot, 26, 49, 152*n.*
Risque, Nancy, 136, 143
Rivlin, Alice, 189, 205
Robertson, Pat, 145, 145*n.*
Rockefeller, Nelson, 66*n.*
  Domestic Council, 66–75
  Eisenhower, 7
  Nixon, 30, 48
  Rumsfeld, 68–71, 74–75
Rogers, William, 26
Romney, George, 20, 43
Roosevelt, Franklin Delano, 1, 5
  Executive Office of the President, 6
  President's Committee on Government
    Organization (PACGO), 7
Roper, William, 165*n.*
  Office of Policy Development,
    165–166, 168
  resignation, 168
Rosenmann, Samuel, 7
Ross, Dennis, 178
Rostenkowski, Dan, 170, 202
Rubin, Robert
  economic policy adviser, 186, 187, 204
  National Economic Council, 190–193,
    196–200, 203, 205, 208, 211
Rumsfeld, Donald, 61*n.*
  Ford: Domestic Council, 64, 68–71, 73–74;
    transition, 58–59; Rockefeller, 68–71,
    74–75; and staff coordinator, 61–64, 73
  Nixon: 24, 39, 43
Rural Affairs Council, 34, 41–42, 44,
    41*n.*, 42*n.*
Rush, Kenneth, 63–64
Russia, 21

Salvatori, Henry, 119*n.*
Schlesinger, James
  dismissal, 106
  Energy, 103, 87*n.*
Schultze, Charles, 89, 94
Schweiker, Richard, 119, 130
Scowcroft, Brent, 156, 159, 174
Scranton, William, 57–58
Sears, John, 112–113, 113*n.*
Segal, Eli, 197, 200
Seidman, Ricki, 186, 187, 204
Seidman, William, 62, 63–64, 75
Shalala, Donna, 183, 202
Shepard, Geoffrey, 51, 53

Shultz, George, 23, 43
Skinner, Samuel
  chief of staff, 169, 174–177
  resignation, 177
Smathers, George, 18
Smith, William French, 119, 133, 119*n.*
Snow, Anthony, 177
Somalia, 173, 201
South Africa, 140
Soviet Union
  Bush, 156, 173
  Carter, 110
  Nixon, 16, 26, 50
  Reagan, 116
Sperling, Gene, 190, 198
State and Local Assistance Act of 1972, 48
Strategic Arms Limitation Talks (SALT II), 142
Steelman, Deborah, 146
Steelman, John, 7
Stephanopoulos, George, 187, 294, 206
  Asst. to the President, 208, 210
  communications director, 186
Stockman, David
  election of 1980, 123*n.*
  Office of Management and Budget,
    123–125, 128–132
  resignation, 136, 136*n.*
Strategic Arms Limitation Talks (SALT), 51
Strategic Arms Reduction Treaty
    (START), 156
Strategic Defense Initiative (SDI), 139
Sullivan, Louis, 157, 170
Sununu, John
  chief of staff, 158–161, 163, 167–169,
    171, 173
  dismissal, 173, 173*n.*
  transition, 155
Svahn, John
  Asst. to the President for Policy
    Development, 132–134, 136–137, 144

Taft Commission on Economy and
    Efficiency, 6
Talent Inventory Program, 84
Tate, Sheila, 146
Teeter, Robert
  election of 1988, 146–148
  resignation, 158
  transition, 150–151, 155
Terra, Daniel, 119*n.*
Thatcher, Margaret, 147

Thompson, James, 174
Thornburgh, Richard, 157, 161–162, 162*n.*
Timmons, William E., 39, 47, 117, 120–121
Torkelson, Jodie, 106
Tower, John, 157
Tower Commission Report, 141–142
Train, Russell E., 23
Transition Advisory Committee, 119, 119*n.*
Truman, Harry, 7
Tuttle, Holmes, 119*n.*
Tutweiler, Margaret, 178
Tyson, Laura D'Andrea, 183, 206

Untermeyer, Chase, 151–153, 159, 153*n.*
Urban Affairs Council (UAC), 26–33, 37–38, 41–44, 55, 42*n.*

Veneman, John, 48
Vietnam War 16–17, 26–27, 45–46, 50
Volpe, John, 20
Voorhis, Jerry, 15*n.*

Waldorf-Astoria Hotel, 18, 66–67
Wallace, George, 15–16, 18
Watergate, 53–54
Watkins, W. David, 187, 204
Watson, Jack
    cabinet clusters, 100–101, 100*n.*
    Cabinet Secretary, 86, 93
    policy development, 99–101, 104
    transition, 83–88, 97*n.*
Watt, James, 119
Webster, William Wendenhall, 206, 208

Weinberger, Caspar
    Nixon: 43
    Reagan: transition, 117, 119*n.*; and
        Defense, 119, 130
welfare reform
    Carter, 82–83, 92, 98, 102
    Clinton, 200, 202
    Nixon, 30
    Reagan, 138
Wellford, Harrison
    Carter transition, 88
    reorganization of Executive Office of the
        President, 93–94
    task forces, 94
Whitaker, John, 49, 33*n.*
Whitehead, Clay, 57
Whyte, William, 57
Wick, Charles, 119, 119*n.*
Widenbaum, Murray, 129
Williams, Margaret, 185, 187, 204, 206
Wilson, William, 119*n.*
Woodham, David, 88
Wrather, Jack, 119*n.*

Yeutter, Clayton
    Counsellor to the President for Domestic
        Policy, 174, 175–177
    Republican National Committee, 174*n.*
    resignation, 177

Zartman, Leonard, 29
Zoellick, Robert, 178
Zoi, Catherine, 190